*Praise for*

## DISTANT GREENS

"*Distant Greens* is an intimate golfing tour that travels to all corners of the planet and brings us into the heart, mind and soul of the game that we all love."

—Rick Lipsey, *Sports Illustrated,*
and author of *Golfing on the Roof of the World*

"These enthralling stories take us to some of the world's strangest golf courses. They are more than travel stories; they are insightful, funny, and often touching human tales that provide new insights on why we play the game. Proves the adage that the quality of sports writing is inversely proportional to the size of the ball."

—Micah Woods, director, Asian Turfgrass Center

"Travels to golf courses where they oughtn't be, visits with some of the most intriguing golfic characters the world over, and never strays far from the reader's heart. A quirky, funny, layered, insightful, beautifully written collection for golfers who ponder the meaning of this ever-fascinating, eternally frustrating, always-satisfying game."

—Daniel Navid, president,
International Golf and Life Foundation

"More than a golf travel book, more than a discourse on the spiritual nature of the game, this collection of insightful (and funny) essays and exceptional reportage explores new vistas about some of golf's most interesting people and places, and gets to the heart of the very reason so many of us love this game."

—Fred Shoemaker,
coach, author, and founder of Extraordinary Golf

"An impressive volume that links reportage on golf around the world with insights on the personal aspects of the game. But what makes *Distant Greens* so important, and a must-read, is how Sochaczewski addresses the role of golf in environmental destruction and, surprisingly for some, how golf can be a force for conservation. He offers new directions that golfers, and golf course owners and managers, should heed, for the good of the game and for the good of nature."
—Jeffrey McNeely, chief scientist,
IUCN-International Union for Conservation of Nature

"*Distant Greens* explores 'inner' golf – the golf of the spirit and heart as well as 'outer' golf – the magic of playing exotic courses and meeting extraordinary people. Equally interesting and important, the book suggests a new eco-spiritual relationship with the game that each golfer can adopt. Essential (and elegant) reading for anyone who loves the game."
—Dennis Cone, founder, Professional Caddies Association

"Paul Sochaczewski has created an exceptional book that gives the reader insights into the internal and external journeys of golf. I'm particularly impressed by the chapters on the psychology of golf. *Distant Greens* is both insightful and thought provoking, particularly since many of the themes in the book relate to how we manage our emotions and how (and why) we create 'core beliefs' based on performance. Why do we make ourselves 'wrong'? Why do we beat ourselves up when we hit bad shots instead of patting ourselves on the back for good shots? What is going on in our complex brains? Golf is a beautiful game, and Paul provides insights into how we might enjoy it more."
—Jennifer K. Jones, consultant in sport and performance psychology, Staffordshire University

# DISTANT GREENS

# DISTANT GREENS

## GOLF, LIFE *AND* SURPRISING SERENDIPITY ON and OFF the FAIRWAYS

## PAUL SPENCER SOCHACZEWSKI

EXPLORER'S EYE PRESS

GENEVA, SWITZERLAND

Some of the articles, essays and profiles in *Distant Greens* were
written over a period spanning several decades; some information
and facts might be dated but the essence of the stories remains
intact.

Earlier versions of many of the articles in this book have appeared
in various international publications, and the author acknowledges
and thanks the editors of the *International Herald Tribune, The New York
Times, Wall Street Journal, CNN Traveller, Geographical, Reader's Digest,
Travel and Leisure Golf, Travel and Leisure, GQ, Destinasian, Golf Vacations*
and other publications for their support.

ISBN: 978-2-940573-22-6

Cover photo: Shutterstock

*Book design by Stacey Aaronson*

Published by:
Explorer's Eye Press
Geneva, Switzerland

Printed in the United States of America

Dedicated to golfers* the world over who strive for a
clean, straight drive and a perfect long putt
on a sloping green.

*Well, not golfers who cheat
(see the chapter "If a Golfer Cheats in the Forest, Does It Count?")
or slow golfers, or able-bodied golfers who ride in carts on flat
courses, or golfers who use cell phones on the course
(see the chapter "Collecting Eco-Golf Karma Points")

# TABLE OF CONTENTS

———◦❧◦———

## I

## INTRODUCTION

*Why would a sane person believe that a tetrachaidecohedron-dimple-pattern could make him happier?*

### Golf or Sex?

———◦❧◦———

## II

## "LEFT SIDE NO GOOD"

*People of the game*

### This Guy Is a Natural

### "My Kid's Gonna Be a Star"

### Induced Labor? That's Real Golf Commitment

### "Left Side No Good"

# V

## GOLF'S PARADOX

*Can golf be green and clean? What might the future hold?*

# VI

## ˙OUT OF THE POISON IVY˙

*Dreaming of truly distant greens*

# I

----◦◦----

# INTRODUCTION

Why would a sane person believe that a
tetrachaidecohedron-dimple-pattern
could make him happier?

# GOLF OR SEX?

## Golf isn't a real sport, is it?

GENEVA, Switzerland

**G**OLF OR SEX?
For many golfers, Augusta National in Georgia, the home of the Masters, is the holy grail of golf courses. St. Andrews, in Scotland, is probably more iconic, but that's a partly public course any golfer can play. Augusta National, though, is a highly exclusive members-only course, so playing it is like dating a movie star – something to dream about but rather unlikely to happen.

But if an average golfer *could* play Augusta National, what would he/she be willing to give up?

A *Golf Digest* survey asked: "You have the opportunity to play Augusta National, but in exchange you will have to abstain from sex for one year. Do you accept the tee time?" Of the respondents, 32 percent of men and 31 percent of women wanted the tee time.

When I was growing up I would never have imagined that golf could have that kind of hold on otherwise normal people.

Paul Spencer Sochaczewski

My earliest golf experience was when I was about ten.
My dad, who was no sportsman, decided that he and I should
engage in some father-son bonding activities – fishing (he
got sunstroke and I got seasick), hiking (my mother made us
crazy with her fears of snakes and poison ivy), and golf. We
played on a municipal course somewhere in the Catskills, in
New York State, using rented clubs and forced to hire a caddie, a teenaged kid probably earning a few bucks for college.
Neither my father nor I had the slightest idea what we were
doing, and we hacked our way around the course for several
un-fun hours.

And then I never picked up a club again until I was in my
late-forties and living near Geneva, Switzerland.

Up to that point I had perceived golf as an activity yearn-
ing to become a sport. Sort of like bowling or shuffleboard.
It was a pastime for old men wearing gawky clothes, a bit like
outdoor gin rummy. I enjoyed real sports – squash and tennis,
and tough wilderness hiking, mountain biking, and skiing.
Sports that made you gasp for air and shout with exhilaration.
Sports they made beer commercials about. But a number of
my otherwise reliable friends were keen golfers, so I took a
few lessons and started to fill my head with swing thoughts –
"swing like it's a baseball bat" was one of the earliest. I bought
spiffy golf shoes; I took a few more lessons and overwhelmed
my head with more swing thoughts. "On the follow through
take a step as if you're walking toward the hole."

I explained to my first golf teacher that I wanted to master the game and didn't care if it took all weekend.

I rented a share in a swish club, where I got scolded for
breaking the dress code.

I acquired more swing thoughts. "Grip the club like a
bird." "Revolve, don't sway." "Hit toward two o'clock."

Before I played golf I had no idea that there were deities
called Golf Gods. I had no idea that there existed a sport
that could turn even the most humorless and straightforward

individual into a sardonic philosopher wearing a bemused half-grin. I had never tasted a Japanese isotonic drink called Sweat.

And even more swing thoughts crashed the party. "Hitch your shoulder like Hideki Matsui." "Don't hitch your shoulder like Hideki Matsui."

What is the addictive attraction of golf, whose professional version, as writer John Tierney notes, "has no body contact, no car crashes, and no cheerleaders." He speculates that golf is the modern version of our Pleistocene ancestors hunting on the savanna, standing on an elevated vista overlooking rolling grassland dotted with trees and water from which the early hunters threw projectiles. In other words, golf is in our genes.

I won't waffle on about how golf has made me a better person, or helped me understand and accept my foibles, or introduced me to fine folks, or helped my social life or enhanced my bank account. What it has done is create a resonance with my interest in yetis and Hobbits.

The study of creatures that are misplaced in time or place is called cryptozoology. I have a slightly beyond-normal curiosity about yetis and their smaller tropical cousins the "snowmen of the jungle." Somehow this has evolved into a parallel interest in what might be called crypto-golf – golf where it oughtn't be. I've played on a "peace and love" 13-hole course in Iran. I've lost balls on the slopes of an active Javanese volcano where the mermaid queen presides. And, in northern India, near the world's highest golf course, I've engaged Tibetan monks in discussions about the meaning of life and why short putts rim out.

There is a certain romanticism in this kind of rugged golf. Writer David Roberts suggests that the pleasure of the proto-golf game called *colfe* that was played by the Dutch, and the early Scottish game we are more familiar with, "resides in the sheer joy of knocking the bejesus out of the ball ... One does not picture a Highland laird or shepherd in the 15th century kneeling over his twenty-foot putt, caddie whispering in his ear. One pictures him clad in a kilt, flailing his oblate pellet 'cross heather and gorse as he tours the nearby hills and lochs: not a good walk spoiled, but a cross-country frolic enhanced."

One golf opportunity that I rejected came from Sir Graham, a hearty Englishman who had legally resurrected the Knights Templar, a prominent and powerful group of medieval Christian noblemen who protected pilgrims on the crusader routes to Jerusalem. He offered me, for less money than the annual dues at my golf club, a "State Sanctioned Hereditary Knighthood," which meant I could pass the title on to my son. It would have been really cool. I would be honored in an investiture involving *apanages* and escutcheons. I'd get to wear a special ring and have use of two castles and the opportunity to buy privately bottled Knights Templar Bordeaux.

As a sweetener, Sir Graham pointed out that he was "just an inch away from receiving United Nations recognition for a new Knights Templar country he was creating, code-named Savantis, and I could have my choice of civic duties. "I don't suppose Chief Pooh-Bah of Golf and Spa Development is still free?" I asked. It was, but I nevertheless turned down the knighthood because in my heart I agreed with my buddy Dan, who observed: "Those guys don't need their own country. They're already on their own planet."

During a particularly bad golf patch I consulted a hypnotist, who made a "think positive" tape that she told me to listen to each evening as I drifted off to sleep. When I told her a few weeks later that my game had actually worsened, the therapist, who was not a golfer, was surprised: "It *should* work. I even put in some subliminal suggestions to hit the ball as hard as you can, like you were a kung fu fighter screaming and leaping through the air."

And yes, golf has taught me a bit about the silliness of life (why, really, would a sane person believe that a tetrachaidecohedron-dimple-pattern of an expensive golf ball could make him happier?).

The first section of this book profiles extraordinary golfers — including characters from Zimbabwe, North Korea, Thailand, and the Chicago Bulls.

The second section examines the psychology of golf — why do we make ourselves wrong, why do some golfers cheat, and the importance of good luck charms.

The third section covers "crypto-golf," which describes golf courses where they oughtn't be — including courses in Mongolia, Borneo, the Amazon, Myanmar, Vietnam, and Iran.

The final section suggests ways to improve the game of golf, notably how golf can be a force for environmental responsibility and steps that could be taken by individuals, golf course owners, and government regulatory agencies.

This is a travelogue. Outer, inner, upside down. A lot of way stations on the road to golfing nirvana. I ran into some unexpected detours, some elegant way stations, some inspiring people, and endless lakes, oceans, swamps, sand, forests, ravines, and cliffs. And once in a while, poison ivy. Which brings me to John Updike, the literate golfer's prose laureate, who suggested that when you hit a lousy shot, shut up and play it out of the poison ivy where you put it. Hit the shot with purpose and a smile.

# II

———◆✕◆———

# "LEFT SIDE
# NO GOOD"

People of the Game

# THIS GUY IS A NATURAL

The world's greatest golfer?
Hint: He rolled a perfect game
the first time he tried bowling.

---

ECHENEVEX, France

IN THE COSMOS OF GOLFING ROLE MODELS, THE HERO-of-heroes might seem a touch unlikely. But this man had one brief shining golfing experience that was Camelot-like in its brilliance.

That golfer was Kim Il-Sung, president of North Korea.

Playing his first-ever golf game[1], the "Dear Leader" shot 34 on the par-72, 7,040-meter, 7,700 yard Pyongyang Golf Course, longer than Augusta National was set up for the Masters. He was 38 under par. Official Pyongyang media reports state that the man referred to as "the sun of the 21st century" aced five holes during that round. Other, more effusive North Korean publications say that he shot eleven holes-in-one in his first try at golf. (A renaissance sportsman, he also reportedly bowled a perfect 300 on his first attempt at that sport.) Regardless of whether the president had five or 11 holes-in-one, the golf pro at the Pyongyang course,

---

[1] The event occurred either in 1991 or 1994 – North Korean sources are unclear – when Kim was either 50 or 53 years old.

Park Young Man, witnessed the round and signed Kim Il-Sung's scorecard, calling his president "a natural." The event was also witnessed by 17 security guards.[2]

Just by way of comparison, Kim's 34 is 25 strokes better than the record-setting 59 shot in PGA tournaments by Al Geiberger, Chip Beck, David Duval, Phil Mickelson, Paul Goydos, and Stuart Appleby, a feat matched by Annika Sörenstam on the ladies tour. "It's like pitching a perfect game," Duval said, except his achievement was rarer – there have been 17 perfect games.

On the other hand, plenty of golfers, including thousands of hackers, have hit holes-in-one.

How hard is it to ace a hole?

Golf statisticians say the amateur odds range from 12,600-to-1 to 33,000-to-1.

On a wintry day over the Christmas break, two friends joined me for a round at my club, Maison Blanche, in Echenevex, France. On a 135-meter (147-yard) par-3, my buddy Dan had a hole-in-one. "Match that" he said to the next golfer. Jeff took a controlled swing and, plop, another ace. Doug Burkert, president of the National Hole-in-One Association, which sells hole-in-one insurance for club tournaments (the premium for a tournament of 100 golfers on a 150-meter (165-yard) hole with a $10,000 prize is $275), calculates the odds of two aces in a row as 150,000,000-to-1. I was hitting next and the pressure got to me; I settled for a par[3].

---

[2] I emailed the North Korean Ministry of Information for confirmation of Kim's achievement, but have not received a reply.

[3] According to Allan Zullo. in his book *Astonishing But True Golf Facts,* something similar happened at England's Trentham course in 1997. Suzan Toft, 72, and Gill Dyke, 62, were playing in a foursome when both aced the 106-meter (116-yard) par 3. A local TV station got word of the feat and asked the ladies to replay their shots for the camera. Incredibly, Toft sank her 5-wood tee shot again. Dyke did not.

According to *Golf Digest*, the odds of a club pro acing are about 6,000-to-1 and for a tour pro about 3,000-to-1.

But for a serious bet, compute the odds of four pro golfers scoring holes-in-one on the same hole, the same day, in a Major, during a breathtaking span of one hour and 50 minutes. The odds are 1.89 quadrillion-to-1. That's a lot of zeroes to describe what Doug Weaver, Mark Wiebe, Jerry Pate, and Nick Price did on the 159-yard (145-meter) 6th hole at Oak Hill Country Club in Rochester, New York, during the 1989 U.S. Open. Curiously, no player who has ever aced a hole during a U.S. Open has ever gone on to win that year's event.

Jack Nicklaus has 20 aces, Arnold Palmer (who, according to writer Chris Rodell, said hitting his first hole-in-one was more exciting than his first kiss) has 19, and Gary Player has 18.

Norman Manley, an amateur golfer from California, has 59 aces, including successive aces on the 330-yard (300-meter), par-4 seventh and the 290-yard (265-meter) par-4 eighth at the Del Valley Country Club., Saugus, California, which is the only time par-4 holes have been consecutively aced.

Texas-based Mancil Davis holds the pro record with 51 holes-in-one and earns his living giving golf exhibitions as "The King of Aces." He says, "They're always asking, 'Is the King of Aces dealing from a full deck?' I love it. Just spell the name right."

The oldest golfer to have a hole-in-one ace was 101-year-old Harold Stilson from Boca Raton, Florida, who on May 16, 2001 hit a 4 iron on the 108-yard (98-meter) 16th at Deerfield Country Club.

The U.S. record for holes-in-one in a single year is 11. Journalist Dave Kindred, writing in *Golf Digest*, describes the fifteen-year-old phenom who achieved this:

> Bradley Farmer is a little guy with a touch of swagger. He's 5-foot-7, 125 pounds. He began playing at age 6, says he broke 80 by age 9, and has shot 61. Out of a wide

stance, he hits it 250 and straight. He's good around the greens. His Hermitage [Golf Course, outside Nashville, Tennessee] handicap is 1.0. He's a basketball guard, a baseball pitcher, and second baseman. His favorite high school class is Bible. He's an only child.

But prodigies sometimes lack credibility, and Bradley Farmer's Achilles heel is that his father was often the sole witness to young Bradley's holes-in-one and that several non-familial "witnesses" have denied having seen the ace in question. It got so bad that after Farmer recorded his fifth ace, the mean-spirited *Tennessean* newspaper wrote: "At Pine Creek G.C. Brad Farmer aced the 196-yard [180-meter] No. 3 with a 5-iron. Witnesses were Papa Farmer ... and Ray Charles." Perhaps tellingly, Farmer went on to play college golf, and his Samford University (Alabama) bio makes no mention of his holes-in-one achievement. Kenny Saunders, a PGA teaching pro at Ocean Dunes in Phan Thiet, Vietnam, who knew Farmer at the Hermitage Golf Course in Tennessee, recalls "I have played with Bradley Farmer on many occasions; my friends and I have often laughed about the Ray Charles story. Also the 61 he claims is also pure fabrication since that would be quite impossible for a golfer of his caliber."

So we continue our search for the real deal, and return to Kim Il-Sung. Any country that can produce a golfing leader like him is a force to be reckoned with, and my advice is that the five countries trying to get North Korea to give up their nuclear weapons had better tread softly.

Maybe Kim Il-Sung's prowess can be attributed not only to his splendid athleticism, but also to his consumption of kimchi. This opens up a whole new field for researchers that could be called gastronomic golf. According to a North Korean official who was briefing a group of Thai journalists, the dragon-breath-producing dish of fermented cabbage seasoned with red pepper, garlic, ginger, green onion, radish, and salted fish "can prevent SARS and bird flu." It's only a logical next step to assume that kimchi can also lead to golf miracles.

Certainly there are signs that the Koreans are doing something right, particularly the women. In May 2016, the Rolex Women's World Golf Rankings shows five (South) Koreans in the top 10. Chalk it up to kimchi?

Will anyone ever match Kim Il-Sung's achievement? Well, the person who came closest was Randi Wilson, a nine-year-old Canadian who got a hole-in-one with her first swing of the club on her first time on a golf course, hitting a 5-iron to ace a 103-yard (94-meter) hole. But she lacked Kim's staying power and afterwards described her desultory round with a sentiment most of us can well understand: "The first hole was great, but the rest of it sucked."

# "MY KID'S GONNA
# BE A STAR"

In Zimbabwe, as in New Jersey, all fathers live their
dreams through their kids.

———※◈※———

## HARARE, Zimbabwe

ON THE PARCHED FAIRWAYS OF THE WINGATE PARK Golf Club in Harare, Zimbabwe, Lewis Muridzo takes a break from his afternoon of lessons and does what fathers everywhere do. He brags about his son.

Tall, articulate, and immaculately dressed, Muridzo pulls out the clippings. His son, Lewis Chitengwa, 25, plays scholarship golf at the University of Virginia. He has won two college championships and finished in seventh place in the NCAA tournament. *Golfweek* magazine selected him as a preseason first-team All American.

And, as Lewis the Senior will tell you with great delight, the boy beat an amateur Tiger Woods by three shots to win the 1992 Orange Bowl World Junior Tournament in Miami.

Nike contracts have started with less.

Lewis Muridzo has paid his dues but never hit the big time himself. He started as a caddie, became Wingate's first black golf club manager, and now is one of the few black golf pros in Zimbabwe. On these fairways-of-dreams, he pushed his children to become champions. A daughter, Rhoda, was offered a golf scholarship to the University of Virginia, but "fell pregnant" and apparently lost her competitive edge. Lewis the Junior is dad's remaining hope.

I've never met the son Lewis Chitengwa, but I can imagine that he picked up his ambition from dad. Lewis the Senior and I played a round together. For three holes I traded pars with the sweet-swinging pro before I got sloppy and he didn't. Concentration is half of golf's oxymoron. The other half is relaxation, which perhaps explains why you have to be either highly focused, or highly neurotic, to play the game well.

Which sounds a bit like the skills needed for fatherhood.

My father bragged about me too, but was never overbearing. He was a dreamer, just as much as I sense Muridzo is.

I sensed my dad's romantic star many times, although he rarely spoke about his inner passions openly – he had the male disease of keeping things to himself. I learned, through his sister, about his Depression-era adventures – bootlegging whiskey off the California coast, drifting, pre-Kerouac, around the States. I don't know how I know, but I know, that he danced and laughed with the French girls after VE day. I saw glimpses of his passion when he would scribble some poetry, or mess around with paints, or go off to Europe on a solitary holiday. But mostly I sensed it when I saw one of his army photos, in which he posed with a trombone in front of a tent. He looked, well, cool. I never heard him play a note, though, and the silent trombone seemed to indicate that my father had put his dreams into a blind trust in order to manage the serious post-war business of raising a family and making a living.

My dad never pushed me; in fact, he rarely said more than "do whatever you think will make you happy." I think he sensed early on that I would have rejected any forced directions to my life, as he had rebelled in his own adolescence against anyone having the temerity to tell him what to do.

And what skills did I possess as a spoiled, skinny, near-sighted kid? I had a successful career in suburban New Jersey high school soccer – I was not bad, but I could never play for Barcelona or Manchester United. I nearly burned down the bathroom while practicing campfire-building skills in the toilet. I was quick and smart and smart-assed, which I suppose might have helped if I had wanted to be a lawyer.

And I always could write. My first major opus, a third-grade play, involved young boys and spaceships and flying bears.

On reflection I see that my father provided support more subtly but just as powerfully as Lewis the Senior offers his son. I remember when I wrote my first article, at the age of 15. I collected ancient Roman and medieval European coins and wrote a convoluted treatise titled "Denarius to Dernier" for an obscure newsletter called the *World Coin Bulletin*. My father helped me take the pictures, setting up a makeshift studio on the kitchen table. Our efforts led to my first sale: $10.

As I grew older and started to explore life, I realized how he was watching me from a distance, gratified that some of his curious and creative genes had found sunlight. Several decades, eighty-odd countries, several books, one son, dozens of mountains later, I like to think that I live a life he would have liked for himself.

My dad's softly-softly approach worked. But Lewis the Senior is taking a more direct approach. Before he put Lewis the Junior on the plane to the States, Lewis Senior insisted that the boy sign a contract making the old man his manager when he turns pro. And his kid, too, is thriving.

Whose way is best? Maybe both, maybe neither. Meanwhile Lewis the Junor is working on his short game, planning to turn pro in the summer.

# INDUCED LABOR? THAT'S REAL GOLF COMMITMENT

## Self-described "Golf Nuts" risk life, liberty, and marital bliss.

——————

## LIMERICK CITY, Ireland

"HONEY, GREAT NEWS ABOUT THE PREGNANCY, BUT would you mind inducing labor so I can play in a tournament?"

Really, how many men would have the audacity to say that to their wives?

Well, Ivan Morris of Limerick City, Ireland, did just that so he could play in the Interprovincial Championships at Royal County Down. His wife agreed, Morris competed, and he won a little trophy.

More important, he earned 1,000 points from the Golf Nuts jury in his successful quest to become 2001 Golf Nut of the Year.

I enjoy golf as much as the next person. I have a few bags stuffed with dusty old clubs, and a few favorite shirts, and many memories. But I doubt I'll ever be elected Golf Nut of the Year by the US-based Golf Nuts Society, a group of duffers that determines the keenest (some might say craziest) golfer in the country.

I sometimes leave work early to get in nine holes before sunset. That minor misdemeanor wouldn't even rate on the Golf Nuts leader board when compared with, say, Scott Houston, 2002 Golf Nut of the Year, who quit his full-time position as executive director of the Monterey (California) Peninsula Chamber of Commerce to follow his dream and become a full-time caddie at Pebble Beach. That earned him 5,000 points. Similarly, 2003 winner Bob Fagan took a six-figure pay decrease to gain an entry-level job with an airline so he could get travel privileges to play more courses outside his driving area.

Fagan, who scored more points in the Golf Nut competition than any other entrant, is among the most tireless golfers. He played 26 top-ranked courses in Michigan during a five-and-a-half day period, while setting four course records and driving more than 1,200 miles (2,000 kilometers); this feat earned him 1,326 points. He played 59 courses in 29 days starting in Miami and finishing in San Francisco (driving solo), and in the process had 19 consecutive rounds in the 60s on courses that he had not before played, including Pebble Beach and Cypress Point. In all, he's played 1,641 golf courses in the United States, arguably the most of any golfer.

Fagan, who has been known to play wearing an army helmet, diving fins, mask, and wet suit, sometimes mis-hits — he has struck all three of his sisters with golf shots, an accomplishment that earned him 300 points. A few mis-hits are understandable, I guess, considering that he's blind in one eye.

I've played plenty of courses when the temperature sizzled, usually carrying my bag, but put my few hours of sweat against Bob Fagan's exploits and it's like climbing a flight of stairs compared to Edmund Hillary and Tenzing Norgay struggling up Everest. At the age of 48, California-based Fagan, who won the Golf Nut trophy in 2003, played six different 18-hole courses in 113°F (45°C) heat in Palm Springs in July in a single day, while walking and carrying his bag on three of the rounds. At Tamarisk Country Club, which was his sixth and final course of the day, Fagan had no drinking water and the clubhouse was closed. "It was like the Burma Death March," he recalls. Another time, needing some aerobic exercise, he played a round on a regulation course in less than 80 strokes and in less than 60 minutes, while carrying his bag containing 14 clubs and umbrella.

Got a love/hate relationship with your clubs? Fagan owns 91 wedges, 14 sets of irons, and more than 80 putters, one of which, when it was "misbehaving," he tied to the trunk of his car and dragged along the highway for the 18-mile (29-kilometer) trip home from the course.

Still, in one memorable round the putter came through for him — Fagan, a two handicap player, broke 80 playing with just that one club.

I take plenty of lessons and buy the occasional instructional video. But I can't compete with 1995 Golf Nut of the Year Brad Bastow, a Michigan cardiologist who hired a live-in golf pro in an attempt to become a scratch golfer. Not convinced that a winter of hitting on a golf simulator would do the trick, Bastow bought a condo at The Vineyards, a private 36-hole country club in Florida, so he and his personal pro could practice. Despite his commitment and expense, Bastow's handicap remained at 13.9.

The great thing about being a Golf Nut is that anybody who is sufficiently obsessed can apply.

Wendi Keen, winner in 1998, proposed divorce to her husband while standing near the 18th green during the final round of an LPGA tournament in Santa Barbara, California.

And Michael Jordan, arguably the most accomplished professional athlete of all time, won the Golf Nut title in 1989; on his Golf Nut application he listed his occupation as "basketball." During the four-month 1989 off-season he calculated that he played an average of 37.5 rounds a month, in addition to his other off-season promotional and business activities. He failed to show for his 1988 National Basketball Association MVP award in Chicago, but he had a valid Golf Nut excuse – he was vacationing at Pinehurst Golf Resort in North Carolina, playing 36 holes and practicing two hours daily. Even better, during the 1993 NBA finals between the Chicago Bulls and the Phoenix Suns, Jordan hid inside a linen truck to escape from the team's hotel before and after practice. The linen truck took him to a waiting car and then to a nearby golf course.

Jordan regularly chose golf over basketball. He withdrew from the 1990 NBA Slam Dunk Contest "due to injury" and played 36 holes the same day. He declined to attend a White House reception for the 1991 World Champion Chicago Bulls and, that's right, played golf instead. When the 1993 NBA All-Star Game was held in chilly Salt Lake City, he skipped "Media Day" and flew to Las Vegas with two other All-Stars to play golf at famous Shadow Creek. When asked why he flew to Las Vegas, he stated that the NBA should arrange to hold All-Star Games only in warm-weather cities so he could more easily play golf.

(Although never elected as Golf Nut of the Year, American football legend Lawrence Taylor, who is a member of the Golf Nuts Society, once played 36 holes on the day of a game, arriving late for a New York Giants' match because the group ahead of his was playing slowly and Taylor didn't want to quit in mid-round.)

Sometimes this Golf Nut business can get a bit, well, compulsive. Steve Smith, 2004 Golf Nut of the Year, has kept his golf stats – including fairways hit, greens in regulation, chips, putts, sand shots, etc., on his computer for every hole of every round he has played since 1993. On winning the title he said, "This is horrible. This is going to be a real problem at home if Paula [his wife] finds out." Paula actually had a pretty good idea such an accolade was coming, considering that on their 34th wedding anniversary, after playing 36 holes of golf with his buddies, she suggested, "Don't you think you're a touch obsessed?" But, to Smith's credit, he never asked her to induce labor in order to make a tee time.

# "LEFT SIDE NO GOOD"

### Asian caddies suggest I might make the shot "in the afternoon of the next life."

———⊰⊱———

## PHUKET, Thailand

"LEFT SIDE NO GOOD," YIM INSTRUCTED ME, POINTing to the lake that paralleled the fairway.

"And right side no good," she continued, gesturing toward a jungle where she feared my slice could easily end up.

My buddy Dan and I were playing Phuket's Blue Canyon, one of Asia's most beautiful courses, and Yim and her colleague Sinjira were our caddies. Thai lady caddies are mostly amiable, often knowledgeable, and sometimes bossy — Yim expected me to follow her instructions.

"Straight, good," she said as I took my last practice swing.

Knowledgeable and charming caddies are largely an Asian phenomenon. It sort of goes with the tropical ambience, along with steamy afternoons, sudden thunderstorms, monkeys and monitor lizards, and gulping an isotonic drink called Sweat.

Except in Japan. In the land of the Rising Sun, lady caddies tend to be older, no-nonsense women, completely covered with hats, shawls, and long-sleeved shirts — like most Asian women, Japanese avoid the sun, feeling that fair skin is more beautiful than a George Hamilton tan. When I played a round at a leading club in Hokkaido, my caddie, whom I shared with three other playing partners, put everyone's bag on a motorized push cart and strode determinedly down the middle of the fairway. These caddies are used to playing with disciplined Japanese golfers who hit everything straight. So whenever I would hit a wayward shot, I had to grab a club from the middle-of-the-fairway caddie, run to my ball, hit a shot, and run back to catch up with the caddie, who by this time had continued her inexorable center-of-fairway march to the green.

All golfers acknowledge that a good caddie can greatly improve the quality and fun of a round of golf. But there is sometimes an intimidation factor. Golfers playing the iconic courses in Scotland are required to take caddies, who are sort of the Anti-Yim – tough guys who have seen it all and who haven't acknowledged a good golf shot since the last sunny day, a wizened guy who hands over a club with a look that seems to say, "I kin be givin you a tennis racket, and it's not going to make a wee bit a difference."

I recalled the story of when Australian actor Oscar Asche was playing a particularly bad game of golf on a Scottish course. After an uncharacteristically good stroke, he risked a casual remark to his weather-worn caddie: "You'll have seen worse players than I am." When the caddie, an elderly Scot, did not reply, Asche assumed that he had not heard and repeated his remark. "I heard ye afore," said the caddie. "I was just considerin ...'"

When they weren't lining up our putts, Dan and I taught Yim and Sinjira to say useful things like "easy as pie" and "don't bet the ranch on it." When I tried a shot that clearly was beyond my level of competence, the women taught us a colorful Thai phrase that roughly translates as "it might occur in the afternoon of the next life."

Then we discussed real life.

"You have many boyfriends?" I asked Yim.

"No, don't want boyfriends," she answered. Sinjira over-heard and corrected, "Yim have five boyfriends."

Yim objected, "No true. Finish with boyfriends."

"And why not? Aren't boyfriends good?"

"No, all boyfriends bad. All boyfriends same-same."

The Thais, living a golfing *sanuk*, seem to have developed the science of caddying to its peak. I've seen groups of six players, each golfer having two caddies – one lady for the bag, and one lady to carry the umbrella, drinks, and cell phone, and to be on call for shoulder massages. This is social golf carried to the extreme, and I find it disconcerting to play behind such a mini-army of generally loud, slow folks. Even worse is to be forced to join such an entourage, with caddies scurrying around the green like puppies on speed.

Which brings us back to that water-hazard-filled hole at Blue Canyon.

I tried to hit it straight. I really did. But I hooked it into the water. Yim looked at me and scolded, "I tell you, left side no good."

# III

## "I CAN MAKE
## THIS PUTT"

Does personal enlightenment lead to more birdies?

# ZEN SHRINE HELPS DUFFERS ANSWER COSMIC QUESTION: WHY CAN'T I PUTT?

Japanese monk invokes Goddess of Holes-in-One.

———◦◦◦———

## ANNAKA, Japan

OLFERS, LORD KNOWS, SEEM TO NEED MORE spiritual guidance then practitioners of other sports. How else could you explain the almost-religious-like belief duffers will place in a Heaven Wood, or the way they mumble the mantra "tetrachaidecohedron dimple pattern" in order to ensure that they will not slice their drives off the first tee during a tournament?

Which is why it is heartening to learn of the world's first Zen shrine devoted to golf.

As reported in *Sports Illustrated*, the golf shrine is the brainchild of 56-year-old Seiko Omi, a "great monk" at the 430-year-old Zenshoji Zen temple at the base of Zuirin Mountain, about three hours northwest of Tokyo. The two-meter tall stone altar Omi designed features Kannon (Kuan Yin in Chinese culture), the Buddhist goddess of mercy. She holds a putter in her right hand, a golf ball in her left. Above thirteen drivers radiating from her head are the Japanese words "hole in one."

Omi, who plays to a modest 36 handicap, hails from a family that has produced monks for twenty generations. He is convinced of his unorthodox approach, saying, "Practicing Buddhist meditation teaches you to calm down and increase your powers of concentration. The power to concentrate is good for everything, especially golf." Omi's ultimate aim is that young golfers who visit the shrine may eventually be moved toward Buddhism.

This softly-softly approach might have aided US golfer Tommy Bolt, known for his graceful swing and terrible temper. Once, after lipping out six straight putts in a tournament, he shook his fist at the heavens and shouted, "Why don't You come on down and fight like a man!"

Golfing legend Sam Snead tried another approach to obtain a golf benediction. Passing through Rome in 1961, Snead was granted an audience with Pope John XXIII. The famous American golfer had been playing poorly and he confessed to one of the papal officials, "I brought along my putter, on the chance that the pope might bless it." The monsignor nodded sympathetically. "I know, Mr. Snead," the priest said. "My putting is absolutely hopeless too." Snead looked at him in amazement. "If you *live* here and can't putt," he exclaimed, "what chance is there for me?"

Like most seekers of cosmic intervention, golfers seem more willing than other mortals to take advice from gurus. Swing thoughts shuffle through a golfer's mind like a shaman's rattle, all of them sensible. But try to remember them all and you'll reach golfing schizophrenia faster than you can say "shift your weight."

John Updike, whose *Golf Dreams* is a bible for literate duffers, summed up the oft-perverse and vaguely ritualistic instructions offered by golf pros, whose status on the golfing hierarchy makes them High Priests of the Links.

"'Hit it with the back of your left hand' was the first swing thought I ever heard," Updike recalls.

He quickly became exposed to dozens of other paradoxical incantations proffered by the golfing sorcerers – "Hit down to make the ball rise." "Swing easy to make it go far." "Finish high to make it go straight."

Increasingly confused by the seemingly contradictory and often arcane advice, Updike recalls:

> I read Arnold Palmer, who said to think of my feet and head as the three apexes of an immovable triangle; your feet should feel like bricks ... Jack Nicklaus put great store in a little rightward cock of the head at takeaway, so his left eyeball and the golf ball were inexorably aligned. Gary Player preferred to think of a core of metal passing up through the middle of his body; he twisted around it like a barbecued chicken on an upright spit. Hale Irwin has lately said he thinks of his hands and the club handle riding down an imaginary flume of water. Sam Snead thinks of waltz time, or of spanking the ball on its backside; his arms, he says, feel like ropes as he swings. Lee Trevino said to accelerate the back of the left hand through the ball toward the target – which puts me back where I began thirty bedeviled years ago.

Michael Murphy, who created California's Esalen Institute and who is acknowledged as one of the founders of the contemporary "personal development" movement, wrote a cult book called *Golf in the Kingdom*. In the novel, an imaginary pro named Shivas Irons, who appears like a specter and offers eternal, sage advice, instructs his disciple to "Let the nothingness into yer shots." One senses the wisdom of a philosophical rabbi, who suggested, "He who would save his life must lose it."

Ah, so in order to play well I must relinquish control. Trust the cosmos. It's hard to do in life and even harder to accomplish when you're facing a tricky 5-iron over water with the match on the line. The message is clear and apparently simple – don't try too hard; relax and become one with the swing, united with the ball. As Updike says, "Play each shot, not the last one, or the next one, but the one at your feet, in the poison ivy, where you put it."

And so it comes full circle for me as well.

Unable to make the pilgrimage to Japan I instead draw a crayon representation of Kannon. I place the representational teeity in a bunker at my home course. I light a joss stick while offering the golf-aiding Kannon a three-pack of new Titleists. "Just a little help with my short game," I intone. "Oh hell, let's go the whole hog." I place a Pebble Beach visor near the altar and add, "And a birdie on that diabolical par-five by the lake. Just once."

# EXTRAORDINARY GOLF IS JUST A CLUB TOSS AWAY

There's always possibility.

---

## PALM SPRINGS, California

EVERY GOLFER KNOWS THIS SCHIZOPHRENIC SCENARIO: You hit a wonderful shot. "Great drive/pitch/putt" exclaims the Optimistic Half of the golfer's brain. "You can do it again."

"No you can't" challenges the Pessimistic Half. And in the self-fulfilling prophecy, the next shot dribbles and ploofs into the lake. Pessimistic Half wins again. You think seriously about heaving your clubs into the same lake that just devoured your Titleist NXT.

Which is why I find it cathartic to fling golf clubs and still feel good about myself.

Welcome to Extraordinary Golf, a new approach to golf that emphasizes personal development and biofeedback. And lots of club throwing. It's an ashram where the meditation is enhanced by hurling junk-shop 4-irons.

Extraordinary Golf is the creation of Fred Shoemaker, a revolutionary disguised as a wholesome golf pro. His goal: to alter the culture of golf from a focus on the techno-fix to an arena for exploration, discovery, and freedom.

Shoemaker, a disciple of the fictional Shivas Irons, the sage Scottish hero of Michael Murphy's classic *Golf in the Kingdom*, proposes that "golf is a creative tool. If you're not creating you're dying. Play a game that's worth playing."

Shoemaker was on the fast track to living the golfing dream. Some 20 years ago, at age 21, he went on the tour. "Everyone said how happy I should be, but I wasn't," he says. "People approached golf, and life, from the point of view that things are wrong. My swing is wrong. My relationship is wrong. Why should we listen to that crazy voice?"

*My* crazy voice becomes apparent early in the school's three-day session. Each of us is videotaped swinging a 5-iron while an Extraordinary Golf pro swings behind us, providing a point of reference of what a smooth swing looks like.

My first swing is not a thing of beauty. "The way you swing tells you how you run your life," Shoemaker explains. Suddenly sobered, I watch my hunched-over posture, my rushed, off-balance swipe.

We are filmed again, this time throwing the club. The club-tossing generates a more fluid swing, more rhythmical than the first.

Our group of 16 students includes golfers with handicaps ranging from scratch to 36. Bill, who has been playing some 30 years, complains that his golf is so erratic that not only is he not having any fun, but he suspects he is no fun to play with. Tucker, a thirty-something businesswoman, wants to transcend fear and simply enjoy the game. Peter, a teaching pro who also plays on the European tour, has come to the school to regain his confidence. "I used to be able to get up and down from anywhere within 50 yards," he says. "Then a coach told me what I *should* be doing and I lost the magic." It's somehow both reassuring and scary to realize that even a guy who hits a drive 300 yards (275 meters) has self-doubts.

Okay, Fred, make us better golfers.

That approach doesn't get me far. Shoemaker makes it

clear that he doesn't think too highly of other golf schools that focus on techno-fixes in which gurus tell the students what they should do. "That's a negative approach," he counsels. "The student is saying, 'I'm no good the way I am. Can you make me better?'" By contrast, at Extraordinary Golf, the recurring mantra is "what's happening?" We are encouraged to feel what's going on. In our bodies. In our golf games. And yes, in our lives. "If you're going to fix your golf game, you might have to change your life," Shoemaker says.

Garry Lester, one of the school's golf pros, explains, "You can recreate yourself playing golf. The future is possibility. Each next shot can be extraordinary. And if you hit a lousy shot, and the voices scream, so what. Just say 'thank you for sharing.'"

"The future is possibility." I've heard that concept phrased dozens of different ways in dozens of personal development workshops. Is this psychology or sport?

During an early-morning course walk, Kim Larsen, a teacher at the school, deliberately shanks a shot into the pond. "What is your reaction when you hit a bad shot?" he asks. Most of us groan and make dark jokes. "Why do people get nervous when they step up to the first tee? Because they're afraid they will repeat a bad shot from the past. That's absurd. Why not create a good shot out of possibility?"

Australian golfer Greg Norman employed this reframing technique to try to break out of the self-doubt hell that he created when he blew a six-stroke lead on the last day of the 1996 Masters. Norman wound up losing by five strokes to Nick Faldo in a performance one journalist compared to a "horrifying slow-motion death that was evocative of an old Sam Peckinpah film." "Let's face it," Norman said, "I'm not the only one who's ever blown a lead. I screwed up badly. [But] I'll just think about the sixty-threes I've shot here. If you keep thinking about the worst round you've ever had in your life, you're going to keep on playing that same round." Which proves that a rosy outlook is good, but you still have to put the ball in the hole – Norman played poorly in his trial-by-fire at the 1997 Masters and missed the cut.

Shoemaker set up a scenario that has occurred to all golfers. "Let's say I hit a lousy shot. The next time I get set to hit a similar shot, I say, 'I can't.' And the irony is that by failing, by hitting a bad shot, I get to be right. It's safer to fail than it is to step into a new identity that I'm not sure of. This costs me my freedom."

We spend our three days on a deep-green golf course in Palm Springs, California, within sight of brown, snow-topped mountains. We jitterbug with our chips, we watch the sparkles on the ball during putts, we notice the ball spin in the air, half in shadow, half in the desert sun. Shoemaker tells us: "If you don't take a chance here, then where?"

Does Extraordinary Golf resemble a revelatory visit to a golfing Lourdes, following which I shout "Hallelujah, I can putt!" and throw away my David Leadbetter instructional videos? Nope, there are no miracles here.

Is my golf swing now consistently smooth and lyrical? Get real. Does every ball go where I want it to? If you ask that question you obviously have never played golf.

But once in a while I sense a ray of possibility. The other day I parred the 18th hole of my club, which involved a classic long, straight drive; a fearless 5-iron over a lake that has gobbled many of my balls; a long, curving uphill putt; and a character-building one-yard putt to finish. I had rhythm and I danced and I heard music. Could I par the hole again? My Pessimistic Half sneers, "Don't bet on it." But hey, there's always possibility.

# THE KEYS TO GOLFING SUCCESS? TRY A RED SHIRT AND THE RIGHT LOCKER

And it never hurts to listen to your mother.

———◦—◦◦—◦———

## LANAI, Hawaii

I WAS PEDALLING UP A HILL ON A RENTED MOUNTAIN bike, sweat evaporating under the fiery sun, glorying in the lunar-like scenery and scolding myself for not bringing enough water. I pedalled toward the Garden of the Gods, a surreal landscape of rocks, twisted lava, and spires of stone, whose earth colors burst into passionate golds and reds at sunrise and sundown. The journey was rougher than I expected, and I was almost alone on the seven-mile (12-kilometer) dirt track that winds through the abandoned pineapple fields. As I neared the ridge, with its fine view of the Pacific Ocean, I sensed, then saw, a companion. It was a small brown and white Hawaiian short-eared owl, a *pueo*, which flew alongside for twenty minutes or so. Here on the sleepy, half-Singapore-sized island of Lanai, so distant in both attitude and lifestyle from the relative sophistication of Honolulu, nature's emissaries carry many meanings, and I wondered what the yellow-eyed owl was telling me.

Omens, superstitions, talismans, magic. And religion. People put their faith in all sorts of rituals, trinkets, spells, and incantations, often through intermediaries – wise men and women who frequently wear peculiar outfits and claim a hotline to the spirits. Golfers are certainly not immune to such beliefs.

People have complicated relationships with owls, perhaps more than with any other bird.

Owls are generally good guys in the ecological sense. They eat mice and rats, which eat farmers' grain – one family of hungry barn owls can consume more than 3,000 rodents in a nesting season.

But they have a mixed image in the spiritual context.

In parts of Europe, owls are associated with insight and good judgment, a belief that can be traced to Ancient Greece where Athena, the goddess of wisdom, had the owl as her symbol.

But in other parts of Europe, as in much of the rest of the world, owls are associated with death. The Romans considered owls funerary birds. In Malaysia and Singapore, they are called *burung hantu*, or ghost birds. The owl symbolized death and destruction among the Aztec and Maya; an old Mexican aphorism says, "When the owl sings, the Indian dies."

Tiger Woods has his own omens and beliefs. You don't need a fortune teller to know what he wears during the final round of every tournament he plays – his good-luck red shirt.

Tiger's crimson polo turns out to be a sartorial statement with a purpose. Like a good Asian son, Tiger's simply listening to his Thai mother, who explains that "red is a lucky color for Tiger. It brings power."

Superstitious? Of course. It comes with the territory when playing golf in Asia.

Shortly after I arrived in Asia, I was invited to play at the Singapore Island Country Club. My friend Guy, a Straits-born Chinese, looked at the key I was given and asked the attendant for a different locker. "Because you're a foreigner," he said, "he gave you a locker with the number four." Guy complained and I was given a locker with an eight. "Eight" is good, I learned, because the number pronounced in Cantonese sounds like the homonym for "prosperity." And "four?" Fuggedaboutit. It sounds like *shi* in Cantonese. "Death."

During my exhausting and exhilarating bike ride with the mystical Hawaiian owl, I got off my bike, sat against a rock, and watched the whales breach in the water far below. I was content and lucky. I was playing Lanai's two world-class golf courses – the Greg Norman-designed Experience at Koele and the Jack Nicklaus-designed Challenge at Manele. I was a guest at two of America's finest hotels. Was this just dumb luck that I arrived at this stage of life, this location on the planet, this degree of health?

Of course I wasn't totally naïve. The logic was simple – I was writing an article for a golf magazine (one that lets its writers accept freebies) and the resorts wanted the publicity. But maybe there was something more supernatural at work. Maybe I did something particularly good in a previous life. I only wish I knew what it was so that I could replicate the good deeds now in order to benefit my next time around. Maybe the owl's wisdom comes from seeing the unseeing, hearing the unheard, from its ability to stalk prey in the black of night, a time when people should be in their beds while spirits roam free. Was the owl a messenger from beyond?

Superstition inhabits that shadow world that includes luck and ritual, and seems to play an important role in golf.

"Golf, perhaps more than any other sport, relies on luck because of the natural environment in which it is played" suggests Steve Cohen, president of the California-based Shivas Irons Society, which promotes the "transformational" elements of golf.

Cohen, who is a gestalt practitioner and workshop leader at the Esalen Institute in Big Sur, California, adds that everyone, not just golfers, needs superstitions because there is so much in the world that is not understandable.

For the big "un-understandables," many people turn to formal religion. There is a fuzzy continuum between the power-infused sacred paraphernalia of formal religions – a crucifix or a St. Christopher's medal for Catholics, or a Star of David or mezuzah for Jews – and the charms, talismans, rituals – a rabbit's foot, a lucky coin, not stepping on a crack – that might be considered secular. Is there really so much difference between Tiger Woods wearing a *sai-sin* Buddhist cord bracelet offered by a monk and Rickie Fowler marking his Pro V1x with "4.13," referring to his favorite passage from Philippians: "I can do everything through him who gives me strength." All part of the same rainbow continuum. Folks might believe in a Hairy Thunderer or a Cosmic Muffin, the Earth Mother or a Good Luck Goblin. They're all ways to seek higher intervention in order to avoid problems and bring luck.

In Bangkok, where I lived for a time, folks often deal with the inexplicable by acquiring amulets. The city, indeed the whole country, is rife with vendors proffering the triple-whammy of prosperity, protection, and salvation. I went to one of my favorite locations, near the Saphan Kwai Skytrain station, where each weekend several hundred dealers – both men and women – sit at little kindergarten-sized tables brimming with talismans. It takes a trained eye to determine which are worth a few cents and which deservedly cost thousands of dollars.

"What's good for golf?" I asked Khun Nok, one of my regular amulet-pushers.

She had never been asked that question and thought for a moment before handing me a popular rectangular amulet, featuring Lord Buddha in a meditation posture.

"Lord Buddha didn't play golf," I said.

"But he can provide the peace of mind you need to succeed."

"What else have you got?"

"Maybe the circular dharma wheel amulet? It represents the continuous cycle of life, one hole after another, one tournament after another."

She showed me a medallion of Luang Phor Bpen, one of the superstar monks in Thailand. The cult of celebrity monks is a curious phenomena in Thailand, and local amulet collectors choose a talisman based largely on its provenance. Everyone knows who the celebrity monks are, and the amulets they have made and blessed command the highest prices. Some of Luang Phor Bpen's amulets show him riding a tiger, like an Asian Buddhist Roy Rogers. "Strong protection, can stop bullets," Khun Nok assured me. "Much good luck."

There is a fuzzy continuum between common good/bad luck habits (not walking under a ladder), good luck charms (rabbit's foot), and these Thai amulets imbued with mythico-spiritual show-business power. All cults, sects, and religions have their own magic-gadgets, of course. While Buddhism in its purest form eschews all forms of desire and grasping for success, the Thai version of this belief system accepts that amulets will help the wearer acquire wealth, be powerful, and collect blessings. How wonderfully Hollywood, and how refreshingly un-Buddhist, that the most powerful (and therefore most expensive) amulets have been blessed by superstar monks, legendary elderly holy men with reputations as big as the secular Western world's Muhammad Ali, Elvis, Einstein and Pelé.

Nok then showed me a fist-sized, disc-shaped *jatukam* amulet issued by a well-known monastery, the same amulet that Thai soldiers in the south of the country have been issued by the government for protection from Muslim insurgents. "You need protection to play golf, don't you?" Khun Nok asked.

Too many options. All made sense yet none of them felt right.

"What about an amulet with Phra Reussi," I suggested, referring to the bearded, goofy-hatted hermit monk who helps people find wisdom.

"Yes, he could help," Khun Nok said. "But so could Phit Tha," she said, referring to the image of a monk covering his eyes, as in "the monkey who sees no evil."

"Isn't it good to see where the ball goes?" I asked.

"Don't be so literal," she scolded. "He covers his eyes so that he is not distracted. Good for focusing. Good for luck."

"Well, not getting distracted is good," I said.

"Then maybe an amulet of Phra Sankachai would be helpful. Khun Nok explained that Sankachai was a ridiculously handsome disciple of Lord Buddha and was so disconcerted by the gazes of lust-in-their-hearts female acolytes that he turned himself into an unattractive fat monk.

I patted my hard-to-control stomach, shaped in that no-man's land somewhere between a six-pack and a keg. No, I don't think a fat, unattractive (but devoted) monk should be my personal golf role model.

I was getting bewildered. I had my two-dollar jeweler's loupe out and was examining the talismans with great intent, but little profound knowledge. I carry the loupe to pretend I know what I'm doing and to garner a touch of undeserved respect from passersby. Not much different to my on-course behavior, actually.

Finally, a dozen other amulets later, she arrived at the amulet I knew she would have to arrive at. Ganesha, the elephant-headed son of Shiva and Parvati. Ganesha, the most beloved and commonly invoked god in the Hindu pantheon. Ganesha, the cuddliest of the gods and one of the most popular in equal-opportunity Thailand, which, although predominantly Buddhist, maintains a deep respect for the Hindu deities.

Ganesha is known as the "remover of obstacles."

I already own several dozen Ganesha statues, collected from Thailand, India, Sri Lanka, Nepal, Myanmar, and Indonesia, and perhaps a hundred smaller Ganesha amulets, all from Thailand. But a guy can't have too many Ganeshi, and I purchased (actually, the correct Thai verb to use in such a transaction is "to rent") a cute little amulet of a Ganesha. He is balanced on one leg and dancing a little jig. Sort of like he just chipped in from off the green to win the U.S. Open.

As a weekend duffer I can fully understand the desire to seek the support of a benevolent outside agency. Why does one long putt go in while another circumnavigates the hole without falling? Why do some horrible slices land on a nice patch of grass with a clear opening to the green, and some wind up behind a cactus? Is this due to luck? And if so, can we improve our luck?

Fred Shoemaker says he creates "an environment in which

a golfer's instincts and awareness lead to the true source of power and proficiency." This doesn't condone cultivating superstitions but sees that they can be beneficial for some golfers. "Superstitions, and the resulting rituals," he says, "are a way for golfers to address their 'self-doubt,' and allow the golfer to be present, instead of worrying about what might happen in the future." He adds that golfers might just be more superstitious than other athletes because "golf is a slow, non-reactive sport (unlike say, tennis), with more opportunities for the golfer's mind to interfere with the action."

Good owl. Bad owl.

In the Hopi Native American tradition, owls are associated with sorcery, and Merlin, the wizard from King Arthur's court, kept the bird close at hand. Perhaps sorcery, an evil twin of superstition, is a good metaphor for our belief in magic and good luck spells.

I find the owl's complex duality – wise and prophetic but also a messenger of death – very Asian. The owl fits comfortably into the cosmos adapted by many Asian societies in which everything has its opposite – yang and yin, male and female, sun and moon, dry season and rainy season, fire and water, Garuda and Naga. Things can best be defined by citing their opposites. There is a light side and a dark side, and these descriptions are made without value judgments. The universe needs both.

Some psychologists suggest that superstitions of any kind can raise stress and anxiety levels.

For Chinese- and Japanese-Americans, the fear of the number four (the same "death" number of the locker I had been given in Singapore) – clinically described as tetraphobia – can be a real killer. Consider this: On the fourth of each month, cardiac deaths for Chinese-Americans and Japanese-Americans spike seven percent compared to other days, according to a 2002 study by a team of scientists at the University of California-La Jolla.

Do superstitions really work in golf? Well, like so many things concerning the human psyche, if you think it will help, it probably does. "A lucky amulet might work because of the placebo effect," Steve Cohen says. "Just because it's not scientific doesn't mean it can't be effective."

I find this a pretty satisfying rationale for a practice that is not at all logical. Anything that silences the monkey-mind when I'm stroking a gotta-make-it putt is worth a try.

Tiger Woods has said that Jack Nicklaus is his role model. Everyone assumes that Tiger's adulation of the Golden Bear is due to Nicklaus's unsurpassed string of victories. But perhaps Tiger also senses an affinity with the Bear's superstitious nature.

Jack Nicklaus carries three pennies in his pocket during each round, explaining, "If I carried only one penny and lost it, I'd be without a ball marker. If I had only two pennies and lost one, and a fellow player needed to borrow one to mark his ball, I'd still be out of ball markers."

Nicklaus always marks his ball with the tails side of the penny up, unlike Paul Azinger who marks his ball with the penny head facing upwards, and always with Lincoln looking toward the hole.

Chi Chi Rodriguez uses three different coins to mark his ball, depending if it is an eagle, birdie, or par putt.

And what about tees?

On par threes, Jack Nicklaus would keep his good tee in his pocket and search for a broken tee on the tee box.

Doug Sanders never played a white tee, believing them to be unlucky. As he stood on the 18th tee box of the last day of the 1970 Open Championship, he needed par to win the Claret Jug. The story goes that Sanders had lost his tee and a playing partner handed him a white one, which Sanders decided to use, against his better judgment, to avoid slowing up proceedings. He went on to bogey the hole, famously missing a three-foot (one-meter) putt, and the following day lost a playoff to Jack Nicklaus (who presumably had three pennies in his pocket).

Some people assert that good-luck charms can work passively. Niels Bohr, the Danish Nobel Prize-winning physicist, had a horseshoe over his lab door, noted David Phillips, the lead author of the La Jolla study about the fatal effects of the number four on Asian Americans. According to Phillips "Somebody said [to Bohr], 'Surely you don't believe this superstition brings you good luck?' He said, 'I don't believe in it, but I'm told it works even if you don't believe in it.'"

So, believe in superstition and it just might work. Don't believe it and, who knows, it might still work. Steve Cohen, the man who explores the philosophy of the fictional savant-golfer Shivas Irons, adds that superstition and ritual are part of "the basis of all religion, and embedded in every culture. Superstition can help you get rid of those things that create anxiety, like a shank in golf."

Superstition is a practice that invokes a higher, or an unknowable force, to irrationally change the outcome of an action or to prevent disaster – think of how we might go out of our way to avoid walking under a ladder.

But when does superstition give way to ritualized behavior that has a grounding in logic? Cohen points out that many people follow religious dietary constrictions, which at one time served a valid hygienic purpose, but which today linger because of a belief in some unprovable, unknowable theology.

And then there's Tiger's dietary regime.

Tiger Woods has a carefully worked out list of foods that he believes make him win – orange and green vegetables, fruit, turkey, baked fish, grilled chicken, skim milk, egg whites, and rice. But he swears that other foods make him lose – pizza, ice cream, cheesecake, roast beef, fried chicken, and soft drinks. Is that blind ritual or just good nutrition?

I'm willing to try anything. Perhaps my own golf game would improve if I carried around a lucky stone my son gave me, or an amulet I got from a wizened medicine man who doubles as a talisman seller on the Philippines island of Siquijor. Couldn't hurt.

And I try to follow the advice attributed to both Gary Player and Arnold Palmer: "The more I practice the luckier I get."

But practice will only get me so far. I think I'll follow Tiger's lead. No more pizza and cheesecake for me before a round. Superstitious? Yeah, probably. So what?

The day following my bike ride and owl encounter, I went snorkeling on the reef just steps from the Manele Bay hotel. I met Florito "Foto" Oliva, the hotel's beach park coordinator. We chatted about the fish I had just seen on the coral reef – a striking dark red rudderfish, a blue parrot fish, a bright yellow tang.

Somehow the conversation shifted into more esoteric subjects – the importance of the planet Jupiter in Polynesian navigation, how Polynesian circumcision parallels Jewish custom, and other esoteric relationships between the Lost Tribe of Israel, Greek mythology, and Hawaiian belief systems.

Recognizing that I was speaking with a wise man, I asked Foto what the *pueo* was trying to tell me. I was curious. Good omen? Bad omen? Or just a bird?

Foto smiled, a rich, wise Polynesian smile. "It's an *aumakua*, a protective spirit of the ancestors," he said. "It's not common that it will fly with someone for so long. It was probably saying 'welcome and enjoy your quiet time.'"

# IF A GOLFER CHEATS IN THE FOREST, DOES IT COUNT?

Rule abuse is rampant among amateurs,
yet professionals exhibit saint-like ethics.

———❦———

## BANGKOK, Thailand

"**P**UT ME DOWN FOR A SIX."
My friend Dan and I looked at each other. "You sure?"
we asked.

We were playing at a Bangkok-area course in a friendly competition (loser buys the beer) against two acquaintances, one of whom was almost elected prime minister of Australia.

The almost prime minister (we called him the Australian Al Gore), who plays off six, had hit his drive into the hazard near the water's edge. We glimpsed him nudge it out of the lakeside rough with his club, bend down and place the ball nicely on a tuft of grass, take another couple of strokes to reach the green, then take a couple of putts.

Six? It was impossible to calculate his strokes because of his rules infringements.

We went on to win the beer, but the incident got me thinking about how widespread cheating is in amateur golf.

In a 2002 survey of 401 high-ranking American corporate executives, 82 percent admitted that they cheat at golf, usually by under-counting strokes or improving their lies.

Why does this bother me?

Golf is the only game where the golfer calls penalties on himself. It is a game of honor, even when the rules appear arcane and silly. For instance, on the course you can move a dead snake out of your line ("loose impediment"), but not a live one ("outside agency").

But life's rules don't have to make sense. They simply *are*. Husbands and wives have their own illogical rules, as do parents, bosses, and the IRS. You choose to follow them, or not.

And, to their credit, pro golfers respect the rules, and by doing so, respect themselves. Maybe it's simply the gentlemanly (yes, ladylike is also an appropriate term) way to behave. Maybe the pros know the rules and the amateurs don't. Maybe it's the knowledge that a spectator or TV camera is likely to pick up any infringement. But consider these acts of character-building behavior.

In 2005 David Toms disqualified himself from the Open Championship at St. Andrews. He believed he might have hit a moving ball when he played the famous 17th, the Road Hole. "It was one of those iffy areas about whether or not a rule was violated and I was the only one that saw it." After the round, he didn't count the two-shot penalty on himself, signed his scorecard, and later reflected that "there was too much uncertainty and thought it was better that I disqualified myself."

Things worked out fine for Mark Wilson who called a two-stroke penalty on himself in the 2007 Honda Classic. During the second round, his caddie Chris Jones accidentally gave Wilson's playing partner Camilo Villegas information about Wilson's club selection during the second round, an infraction of the rules that calls for a two-stroke penalty. Wilson had hit his hybrid and Villegas said to Wilson's caddie,

"What is that?" According to Wilson: "My caddie just happened to turn around and say, 'Oh, it's an eighteen-degree,'
and I'm like, I don't think that's right."[4] Nevertheless, Wilson held on to win in a playoff for his first PGA Tour victory.
Perhaps virtue is rewarded by some cosmic rules adjudicator?

Pundits say, "It's not a principle until it costs you money."
Brian Davis of England will earn karma credit for his princi-
ples for many years to come.

Immediately after hitting his pitch from the hazard near
the 18th green at Calibogue Sound, South Carolina, during a
playoff with Jim Furyk, Davis summoned a rules official. At
stake: the 2010 Verizon Heritage title, which would have
earned Davis his first PGA Tour victory and a two-year Tour
exemption.

Davis had ever-so-slightly nicked a reed during his
backswing. Barely moved it. It could have been a little gust
of wind. To the naked eye, it was virtually invisible. But not
to Davis, who called a two-stroke penalty on himself that
cost him the tournament and $411,000, the difference be-
tween the first and second place prize money.

What Bobby Jones said in 1925, after calling a similar
penalty on himself, still holds today: "You may as well praise
a man for not robbing a bank."

High-schooler Zach Nash was shocked when, a couple of
hours after winning a junior Wisconsin PGA tournament, he
discovered he had one too many golf clubs in his bag. But
rules are rules, and the 14-year-old from southern Wisconsin
made a decision that might surprise some people: he disqualified himself and surrendered his medal.

---

[4] Of course Villegas never should have asked.

During the second stage of a 2009 PGA Tour qualifying tournament in Texas, J. P. Hayes discovered that on two shots on one hole, he had unwittingly used a prototype golf ball not approved for competition by the United States Golf Association.

A full-time spot on the PGA Tour in 2009 was on the line, and if Hayes had simply kept his mouth shut, no one would have known. But Hayes, honoring the tradition of a game where the players police themselves, turned himself in and was disqualified.

"It's extremely disappointing," Hayes said, according to the Milwaukee *Journal Sentinel*. "I keep thinking I'm going to wake up and this is going to be a bad nightmare."

J.P. Hayes says anyone else on the PGA Tour in his situation "would have done the same thing."

According to Don Van Natta, author of *First Off the Tee: Presidential Hackers, Duffers and Cheaters from Taft to Bush*, the worst presidential golf cheats were Richard Nixon and Bill Clinton. According to Van Natta, Clinton even had the temerity to blatantly cheat during a round with Van Natta, knowing that the writer was there to document the president's lack of ethics on the course.

Combining cheating with insensitivity, George W. Bush was teeing off when some journalists asked for his comments about a suicide bomber who had just killed nine people on an Israeli bus. "I call upon all nations to do everything they can to stop these terrorist killers," the president intoned. "Now watch this drive." Bush hit a ball into the rough, grabbed another ball and hit his mulligan straight.[5] "Hard this early in

---

[5] Neither "gimme" nor "mulligan" are mentioned in the rules of golf.

the morning to loosen up," Bush said to the scribbling reporter.

As I write this in mid-2016, it looks like Donald Trump has a chance to become president. If so, he would take the mantle of least-honest golfing president.

Mark Mulvoy, the managing editor of *Sports Illustrated*, was playing with The Donald when Trump arbitrarily placed his ball ten feet from the hole. "Donald, give me a f--g break," Mulvoy said. "You do not lie there." When the story was published, Trump first denied having ever played with Mulvoy, saying, "I don't even know who he is." Trump also denied the story saying, "I don't drop balls. I don't move balls. I don't need to ... There's [sic] very few people that [sic] can beat me in golf." Then Trump changed tack and added, "Ahh, the guys I play with cheat all the time. I have to cheat just to keep up with them."

Rick Reilly, a noted golf writer with *Sports Illustrated* and commentator for ESPN, played a round with Trump and noted that "He couldn't have been more gracious or more fun." But Reilly added that Trump wrote down scores he hadn't achieved, conceded putts to himself by raking the ball into the hole with his putter instead of striking it properly, and taking "the world's first gimme chip-in." Reilly added, "When it comes to cheating, he's an 11 on a scale of one to 10." Trump replied, "I always thought [Reilly] was a terrible writer ... I absolutely killed him, and he wrote very inaccurately." Reilly had the last word: "Golf is like bicycle shorts. It can reveal a lot about a guy."

Boxing champ Oscar de la Hoya said Trump broke the rules numerous times in the two holes the men played together.

On one hole, according to de la Hoya, Trump's first shot landed in the water. The next went out of bounds. The third sliced back into the water. And the fourth was lost to the surrounding bushes. Yet Trump drove his cart to the middle of the fairway and declared that the ball lying there was his first drive and played from there. Similarly, on the next hole, a par-3, when de la Hoya saw Trump's tee shot sail into the bushes, Trump "found" his ball three feet from the hole, then picked it up, claiming a gimme.

Actor Samuel L. Jackson played golf with Trump, along with actor Anthony Anderson. Jackson said he and Anderson "clearly saw [Trump] hit a ball into a lake at Trump National in Jersey – and [Trump's] caddy told him he'd found it." Trump played the ball from the fairway, without penalty or chagrin. When the story became public, Trump replied that he had never played with Jackson and did not know him, and added that Jackson's work in the film *Pulp Fiction* was "boring."

(Yes, it gave me pleasure to write this section.)

So-called local rules usually reduce punishments for golfers.[6] Sometimes, though, the committee will put in local rules that make the game even harder. During World War II, as German planes flew raids over London, the stiff-upper-lipped officials of London's Richmond Golf Club demanded a one-stroke penalty for any member wishing to retake an errant shot "affected by the simultaneous explosion of a bomb." (Players

---

[6] For example, a shot that lands in a groomed flower bed is generally considered a free drop.

were also asked to remove shrapnel from the fairways to prevent damage to the mowers.)

The stigma of being called a cheat is as persistent as malaria in the blood.

In 1985, when he was 22, Vijay Singh was banned from the Asian tour by the Southeast Asia Golf Federation for modifying his scorecard in the Indonesian Open by one stroke so he could make the cut, an allegation Singh denies. As a result, Singh spent two years in the wilderness, working as a club pro at two courses in Malaysian Borneo.

Singh went on to become one of the world's best golfers. When he won the 2000 Masters, John Garrity, writing in *Sports Illustrated*, resurrected the cheating allegation, asking, "What's a fair sentence for a youthful indiscretion?"

Garrity concluded that "he's a great golfer" and the media should "cut him some slack for a youthful indiscretion and let the man's brilliance be the standard-bearer for his career."

Ernie Els came to the defense of Singh and attacked Garrity for even raising the cheating allegation. "Why would someone say that about Vijay as he triumphed in the Masters?" Els asked. "Why would SI's article on the first major of the 21st century not confine itself to Vijay's magnificent victory? Why instead did the writer dredge up an unsubstantiated allegation about an event that may or may not have occurred 15 years ago?"

But like a cold sore on a beautiful face, the allegation refuses to completely disappear. As Garrity notes, "The cloud of Jakarta hangs over Singh." Or, as one prominent American golfer sniffed, "Once a cheater, always a cheater. Golf has a long memory."

Maybe it was a good thing that my Australian acquaintance never became leader of his country. Does any country need a leader who doesn't play fair dinkum?

# NEGATIVITY LAND

Why do we take such delight in golf's screwups
instead of the great moments of success?

———◈———

## EVERY COURSE, Everywhere

A GOLFER FACES MORE DARK SIDE MOMENTS THAN Luke Skywalker.

We take a morbid delight when golf legends screw up. And we wallow in our own masochistic moments of crash and burn.

Why is that? Why can't we spend more energy applauding and internalizing the great shots? Why do we revel in the dark instead of savoring the light? Something is upside-down. Our brains seek the shadows.

Neurotic and unproductive as it may be, it *is* great fun to recall golf's most memorable disasters.

◈

At the 1939 U.S. Open at Philadelphia Country Club, Sam Snead, needing pars on both the 17th and 18th to beat Byron Nelson, bogeyed 17. Requiring a birdie four on 18 to win, but only a par to make a playoff, he hooked his tee shot into the rough. His topped 2-wood bounced into a bunker 110 yards (100 meters) short of the green. His 8-iron thudded into that bunker's sodded face. His fourth shot dribbled into another bunker. On five, he three-putted for an eight, finishing fifth.

Although he won 48 events on the Japan Golf Tour and was once ranked fifth in the world, Japanese golfer Tsuneyuki "Tommy" Nakajima is best known for his never-ending visit to the Road Hole bunker at the 17th at St. Andrews. It was the third day of the 1978 Open Championship and Nakajima, tied for the lead with Tom Weiskopf, was happy to be on the green in two. But his putt rolled past the hole and off the green into the hazard. Trying to hack out, and trying again, and again, Nakajima took four strokes to extricate himself and ultimately had to write a nine on his scorecard, which led the British tabloids to christen that bunker the "Sands of Nakajima." When asked if he'd lost concentration Nakajima replied, "No, I lost count."[7]

At the 1966 U.S. Open at Olympic in San Francisco, Arnold Palmer had a seven-stroke lead over Billy Casper going into the last nine holes. Palmer decided to play aggressively and try to beat the U.S. Open scoring record held by Ben Hogan. Palmer had a few implosions, Casper didn't, and Casper won the next day's playoff, 69 to 73. *Sports Illustrated* called Palmer's collapse "one of the great debacles of modern times, comparable to the Italian retreat at Caporetto, the Edsel car, and Liz Taylor's *Cleopatra*."

---

[7] It was a tough year for Nakajima. In the Masters several months earlier, he shot a 13 on the 13th hole at Augusta National, a score that remains the record for that particular hole.

Most golf fans remember Jean Van de Velde's go-for-broke attitude on the 18th at the 1999 Open Championship at Carnoustie. The French golfer needed just a six on the par-4 final hole for victory. After a so-so drive, he should have, in retrospect, laid up in front of the Barry Burn, then hit a short iron to the green, which would have left him with three putts for the victory. Van de Velde, however, thought he had a good lie in the rough and he went for the green. But his 2-iron second shot hit the grandstand next to the green, then bounced off the rocks on Barry Burn and into the creek. What happened next was one of the iconic images of professional golf – Jean Van de Velde taking off his shoes, rolling up his pants, sporting a Huck Finn-like grin, and thinking about playing out of the water. He reconsidered and took a penalty drop. He still could have pitched onto the green and one-putted for victory. But his fourth shot landed in the greenside bunker. He splashed out to about two meters (six feet). In an eerily silent moment, he hit arguably the gutsiest shot of his tournament – he made the putt to put him into a playoff with Justin Leonard and Paul Lawrie, the ultimate winner. When Val de Velde went for the post-game press conference, he noted the serious and downcast looks of the journalists. "What is the matter?" he asked. "No one has died."

We've all faced a risk-reward tee-shot over a lake to a dogleg fairway. How much lake are you willing to try to carry? On the 543-yard (497-meter) 6th hole at the 1998 Bay Hill Invitational in Orlando, Florida, John Daly, one of the tour's longer and braver ball strikers, hit driver and aimed his shot at an ambitious angle. Splash. He took his penalty drop on the forward tee and for his third shot, hitting 3-wood, tried to cut off even more of the dogleg, a shot of about 300 yards (275 meters). Splish. And another 3-wood. Splash. Spectators began chanting "Tin Cup," referencing the movie in which a stubborn Kevin Costner hits one ball after another into the pond while trying to win the U.S. Open. Splish. Splash. Splish. Daly cleared the water on his seventh swing, but it plugged in the hazard, plop. He took a drop, and his 6-iron toward the green landed in the rocks and ricocheted into a bunker. He blasted out and two-putted for an 18.

And who can forget Australian golfer Greg Norman's flaming implosion when he blew a six-stroke lead on the last day of the 1996 Masters. Norman wound up losing by five strokes to Nick Faldo in a performance one journalist compared to a "horrifying slow-motion death that was evocative of an old Sam Peckinpah film."

Hoping for the universe's longest golf shot, in 1971 Apollo 14 astronaut Alan Shepard hit a golf ball on the moon with a 6-iron. The moon's gravity, just one-sixth that of earth, was on his side, but he neglected to factor in the bulky space suit, which hampered his swing. Swinging with one hand he caught the ball fat and watched it dribble about as far as an earth-bound sand wedge. Instead of uttering a historic sound-bite like Neil Armstrong's "one giant leap for mankind," Shepard muttered, "Got more dirt than ball. Here we go again."

These grisly moments have taken their toll. Sam Snead, who lost the U.S. Open in 1939 to Byron Nelson, never won the tournament. (He suffered another indignity when, at the age of 89 and suffering what his son called "stroke-like symptoms," Snead shanked his 100-yard (93-meter) drive when he served as honorary starter of the Masters. That would be bad enough, but his errant drive hit a spectator on the nose and broke the man's glasses. But the fan was otherwise unharmed and was given a Masters green jacket for his pain.) Arnold Palmer, only 34 at the time, never won an eighth major title following that afternoon at Olympic when he blew a seven-stroke lead over the last nine holes. Since his crash at the Masters, Norman never won another a major. And Van de Velde? He never became a great, just a guy who had fifteen minutes of fame when he waded into the stream and thought about hitting out from an impossible lie.

And Alan Shepard? He hit his mulligan-on-the-moon, a "one-handed chilli dip" he called it, which he claimed traveled "miles and miles and miles!" The astronaut later estimated his shot as just 200 to 400 yards (182 to 365 meters), which is still pretty good for a one-handed 6-iron.

Crash-and-burn anecdotes of the pros are endlessly intriguing, and I wonder why that is. Certainly there is some *schadenfreude* involved, the almost illicit pleasure that "even the pros can mess up big time." But I think it's more to do with the fact that amateur golfers (yes, me) always screw up shots and make stupid mistakes, and this leads to a certain unlikely brotherhood with the likes of Arnold Palmer and Sam Snead and Tommy Nakajima.

Nevertheless, we always live to play another day.

Logically we must accept that we're not perfect, that we're as likely to hit some bad shots as the sun is likely to rise tomorrow. That's life, that's sports.

But what I don't understand is why golfers put so much energy into remembering, and thereby encouraging, lousy shots instead of glorying in a finely hit drive, a high pitch that lands softly next to the pin, a long, snaking putt that swirls into the cup?

We relish the mistakes instead of cheering the much

more numerous good shots. It's backward, it's contrary, it doesn't make any sense and it's self-destructive.

Examine the memorable disasters of the professionals. They all take place at the end of tournaments, when the unfortunate golfer snatches defeat from the jaws of victory. But to get to a leading position at the end of a tournament means the golfer had to play exceptionally well in the previous three rounds. He had to make some memorable long putts, he had to chip in once in a while, he had to hit the fairways and avoid the bunkers. But everyone ignores those highlights and focuses on the end-game mistakes. Curious.

Pundits say that you only learn about yourself during times of adversity. Maybe, but why do we dwell in Negativity Land? Why can't our brains do a better job of imprinting the physiological and emotional pleasure of a shot hit pure and straight?

Such negativity can have implications that go beyond a sliced drive. The respected 1992 Framingham Heart Study noted that women who believe they are at risk from heart disease are 3.6 times more likely to die from heart attacks than those with identical risk factors, but who lack the belief. Negativity as a self-fulfilling prophecy.

Research indicates that the more setbacks people have, the more resilient they become. Roxane Cohen Silver, a psychologist at the University of California, Irvine, says, "each negative event a person faces leads to an attempt to cope, which forces people to learn about their own capabilities." Although Silver was talking about traumatic events like divorce, the death of a loved one, or being in a natural disaster, perhaps on a lesser scale the same could be said of golf trauma.

So, this wallowing in self-abuse is vaguely Nietzschean; "the golf disaster that does not kill me makes me stronger."

In the first round of the 2016 Open Championship at Royal Troon, Phil Mikelson had a five-meter (16-foot) putt on the 18th hole. If he made it, he would become the first man to score 62 in a major championship. His playing partner, Ernie Els, who was lying closer to the pin, putted first in order to give Mickelson the spotlight for his historic putt. Mickelson's putt was on-line all the way, the crowd was starting to cheer, and Phil smiled and started to walk toward the hole. But at the last moment, the ball veered a centimeter to the right, lipped out, and made a half-circle tour around the hole. Mickelson had to "settle" for a 63, becoming the 28th player to score that low in 437 major championships.

This is a classic case of remembering the mistakes instead of reveling in the great shots. The media were full of stories about Mickelson's "tragic" miss. Mickelson himself said he "felt like crying," and said, "There's a curse because that ball should have been in. I didn't believe in the golf gods, but I do now."

And every article on Mickelson's painful miss (or was it a curse?) focused on how other great golfers had similarly missed what they thought was their final putt. Jack Nicklaus missed a one-meter putt for 62 in the U.S. Open at Baltusrol, later saying that he "totally choked." As Tom English of the BBC pointed out, "When did Nicklaus ever choke?" In the 2007 PGA Championship, Tiger Woods hit a putt for 62 that went halfway down the hole and inexplicably popped out.

My point is that by focusing on the missed putts to make history, the players and the media were celebrating the mistakes and ignoring the fact that prior to that almost-historical putt, the player had to play 61 prior holes that were mostly terrific. They had forgotten the great drives, the precise approaches, the sand shots that landed softly near the hole, the heroic saves from the rough, the long curving putts that went in. Everybody had focused on the "wrong"; no one had focused on the "good." Same dynamic as when a club golfer beats herself up for hitting a drive into the lake. She makes herself "wrong" instead of remembering and imprinting the good shots.

The conclusion of the 2016 Open Championship? In the final fourth round, Phil Mickelson and Henrik Stenson played one of the most enthralling matches ever seen in a major. Like gladiators each punched hard, the other took the blow and countered with an equally impressive shot. Each player made dramatic long putts, and each recovered from potentially disastrous lies. At the end, Mickelson shot an impressive 65. Stenson shot the 29th 63 ever recorded in a major, and beat Mickelson by three shots.

I'm trying to find a good metaphor. Dwelling on a bad (or unlucky) shot is like picking at a scab – ultimately the wound becomes infected and what was formerly a minor irritation becomes something more serious.

I have developed a method for imprinting good shots. I won't bore you with it (it's complicated), but it involves repeating my pre-shot routine after a good shot, re-visualizing the shot and context, and writing it down for later review.

Can any good come from meltdowns?

Probably the most sadistic (and masochistic, since participants had to nominate themselves as bad golfers) magazine promotion occurred in 1986 when *Golf Digest* held a competition to find America's "Worst Avid Golfer." The winner: Angelo Spagnolo, then a 31-year-old grocer from Fayette City, Pennsylvania. *Golf Digest* invited Spagnolo and a few other self-designated bad golfers to compete for the title in a televised event. The darkest moment came at the famous 132-yard (120-meter) 17th at TPC Sawgrass, where the golfer has to hit to what is termed an island green (which is really a peninsula, and the distinction is important).

Spagnolo put 27 balls in the water – his iron shots, even from the drop area, flew like rifle shots, rarely more than waist high. Ultimately and reluctantly, on the advice of his caddy and the urging of the TV producer, Spagnolo putted along the winding sandy path that connected the tee with the green. He got on the green in 63 and three-putted for a 66. "One of the TV networks gave me uncut footage of that hole," Spagnolo recalls. "It was like watching my fingernails get pulled out." Journalist Peter Andrews noted, "Let me tell you something about Angelo Spagnolo. In enduring perhaps 40 minutes of public humiliation, he did not wince or cry aloud. At no time did a single whispered blasphemy escape his lips. He took a 66 without a curse. Angelo Spagnolo has either the makings of a Christian saint or the most limited vocabulary of any man who has ever played golf." Spagnolo remembers the support he got from strangers: "Hundreds of people told me I gave them hope. It didn't make me feel any better about the way I played, but it made them feel better about the way *they* played. And I figured that was good for golf."

# IV

---❖❖---

# DISTANT GREENS

Crypto-golf;
golf where it oughtn't be

# (NOT) ERUPTING WITH THE MERMAID QUEEN

The "love affair for the ages" continues on a golf course perched on the shoulder of a volcano.

———◦❈◦———

## MOUNT MERAPI, Indonesia

TO MY UNTRAINED EYE, THE 2ND HOLE AT MERAPI Golf Course looked like just another pretty, well-maintained hole on this attractive mountain course in central Java.

But in golf, as in life, few things are as simple as they appear.

Sukirman, the director of the course, had told me that a spirit is sometimes seen in the small stream that runs through a glade near the dogleg of the 2nd hole. "It has the body of a serpent and the head of a woman," he says. "Lots of people have seen it."

I examined the location and walked carefully down slippery stone steps. No spirit in sight, but as every ghost hunter knows, absence of proof is not proof of absence.

Later in my round, I asked my caddie Murwani, who lives in a nearby village, whether she had ever seen anything *aneh* (unusual) on the course. At first she was reluctant to tell me her story, but when we reached the fairway of the par-5 17th hole, she explained that five years earlier she saw an unusually large brown and black snake resting on a flat rock near the pond that flanks the fairway. It had a body "as big as a man's thigh" and was maybe 25 feet (seven meters) long. The head appeared human. As Murwani approached, the snake slithered into the water. I asked around and learned that several gardeners have also reported seeing a similar snake, and one observer was certain that the python-like creature he spotted had the head and body of a woman, sort of like a reptilian mermaid.

In golf, as in life, few things are as simple as they appear.

Wildlife sightings aren't terribly rare on golf courses, but this anthropomorphic snake was likely an avatar of the spirit that rules over this revered region.

Here's where things start to get a touch complicated.

Mount Merapi (in Indonesian *Gunung Merapi*, literally "fire mountain") is one of the most active and dangerous of Indonesia's 127 active volcanoes. The volcano is sacred, partly because volcanoes have the unpredictable dualistic power to destroy and then create — the volcanic soil near Merapi is extremely fertile, and after an eruption, even when the volcano is still active, local farmers flock back to their homesteads where they are assured of a good crop.

Pre-industrial people have always sought explanations for difficult-to-understand natural disasters. If you don't understand plate tectonics, for example, you might be tempted to believe that the spirits that live in a sputtering volcano are somehow upset, and must be appeased if order is to be restored.

Such high-level mediation is often the responsibility of the king, who is charged with maintaining a balance between the mundane world of his subjects and the supernatural world of the deities. The king, with assistance from seers, soothsayers, shamans, oracles, and priests, must ensure that it rains, but not too much. That the sun shines, but not continuously. That the rivers run heavy with fish, that wildlife is plentiful, and that plagues detour around the kingdom.

Which brings us to Kanjeng Ratu Kidul, the Queen of the Southern Ocean, the Mermaid Queen.

Apologies if this gets a bit complicated, but one of the delights of visiting Java is the challenge of trying to understand the complex Javanese view of the universe.

If you were to draw a line 55 kilometers (34 miles) due south of Mount Merapi, you would come to the beach of Parangkusumo, near Parangtritis. The sea churns, there is a sharp drop-off, and unwary bathers can be pulled by riptides out to sea.

But most visitors do not venture into the water knowing that the Southern Sea is the home of Kanjeng Ratu Kidul, the Queen of the Southern Ocean. This powerful goddess was the consort of Senopati, the 16th-century prince who founded the Mataram Dynasty; she continues her role as spiritual consort of the monarchs of the current royal lines of Surakarta (Solo) and Yogyakarta.[8]

It's a complicated story, but simply put, Senopati spent three nights at Kanjeng Ratu Kidul's underwater palace, where she taught him the joys of lovemaking and the intricacies of good governance. She gave him a great gift – not only

---

[8] For more on the influence of Kanjeng Ratu Kidul, see my book *Curious Encounters of the Human Kind – Indonesia*.

did she promise to support him in his (successful) efforts to start a new kingdom, but she promised to support all future rulers of the Mataram Dynasty.

And lying almost midway on the axis between Mount Merapi and Parangkusomo, one finds the *kraton* (palace) of Sultan Hamengkubuwono of Yogyakarta, a descendant of Senopati.

All Javanese from this region acknowledge Kanjeng Ratu Kidul as Queen of the Southern Ocean. She is a spirited entity who sometimes appears as an old woman, sometimes as a beautiful maiden. Her favorite color is green, and men who dare to wear this color while visiting the beach are living dangerously. And more to the point for this story, she has no patience with people who disrespect traditional Javanese rituals and who exhibit unseemly behavior.

Some people feel that her powerful dominion (which includes armies, officials, and a vast palace) covers not only the Southern Sea, but also Mount Merapi, which she uses as a cosmic weekend retreat. I have spoken with seers who firmly believe that the numerous eruptions of Mount Merapi are evidence that Kanjeng Ratu Kidul is displeased with the state of the world (say, rampant corruption or decline in morality) and sending a message to wayward Javanese to behave properly.

However, some people believe that Mount Merapi is home of a parallel, but considerably less powerful, spiritual kingdom, supervised by a female spirit named Nyai Gadung Melati.

For the sake of this chapter, I'll acknowledge Kanjeng Ratu Kidul as having dominion over Mount Merapi.

Merapi Golf Course, a professional-length par-72 setup designed by five-time British Open champion Peter Thomson, is set on the flanks of Mount Merapi, near the royal cities of Yogyakarta and Solo.

So it was no surprise to the villagers around the golf course area when Mount Merapi gurgled a minor eruption on November 30, 1994, the day construction of the golf course began. The open-minded Javanese chose to regard this as a positive sign that Kanjeng Ratu Kidul was blessing the venture, ignoring the fact that eight days earlier, the volcano had erupted without warning and killed 60 people.

And, to add a touch more mystery, consider that the Sultan of Yogyakarta plays at Merapi Golf Course every week. While he is on the course it never rains, even on the cloudiest, most threatening days.[9] But as soon as he gets into his car, the skies open up. The Mermaid Queen saying farewell, until next week?

I invited K.R.T. Hardjonagoro, the regent of the susuhunan's palace in Solo, to dinner. While nibbling some of the fried chicken for which Central Java is famous, he told me an extraordinary story that occurred in 1966 when Sultan Hamengku Buwono IX (of Yogyakarta) presided over the opening of the Samudra Beach Hotel, on Java's southern coast, which of course is Ratu (Queen) Kidul's home territory. "In the morning, a few hours before the event, a local *lurah* (village headman) asked for an audience with the sultan," Hardjonagoro explained:

> The old man told the sultan that he had had a dream the previous night in which a lady said she wanted her offerings. She was dressed in green.

The sultan, of course, knew that the old man had

---

[9] Sukirman, director of Merapi Golf, discounts this claim.

seen Ratu Kidul. His highness thanked the humbled old man but explained that he would not make an offering since he was attending the hotel opening in his civilian capacity as minister of defense, and he wanted to separate the affairs of the state from the mystical duties of the palace.

We ordered more chicken and Hardjonagoro continued:

I was outside, near the pool, when the sultan said good-bye to the well-meaning old man. A bit later I heard the sound of a locomotive. The noise increased until it sounded like ten locomotives were coming toward the beach-front terrace where we were enjoying the hotel's hospitality. Then a huge tidal wave erupted from the sea, which had been calm. It washed away the hotel's buffet table and soaked all the visitors. Some trees were knocked down. Someone ran to tell the sultan what had happened, and realizing what had occurred, the sultan put on his ceremonial clothes, said his prayers to Ratu Kidul, and made the appropriate offerings. The sea was calm once again.

I was incredulous. Hardjonagoro showed me the photos. I said "come on," or something equally un-Javanese. Instead of arguing, he simply told me to go to the hotel and ask for room 308. Sometime later, I did. This, it turns out, is the room in which Sultan Hamengku Buwono IX made peace with the easily irritated Mermaid Queen. It is kept locked and reserved only for her. For a tip, hotel staff will allow people access so they can pray to the Queen of the Southern Ocean. It is a good business.

It pleased me to think that the offerings to Kanjeng Ratu Kidul made by the course developers and local inhabitants at the beginning of construction of the Merapi Golf Course had been accepted. The site had been a desolate and unproductive region of scrub and 1,400-year-old lava. It now harbors butterflies and dragonflies, provides employment for 450 local people, and the course developers have installed irrigation systems and fish ponds for the neighboring villages.

When I first played Merapi Golf, in the late 1990s, Mount Merapi was gurgling poison gas and burping lava, and volcanologists predicted an eruption. But in spite of these geological events, the Merapi Golf Course has never been directly hit. Does Kanjeng Ratu Kidul protect the course? I'd like to think so, but it doesn't bear overanalyzing. I remember what Sultan Hamengkubuwono IX had told me when I questioned him about his relationship with the Mermaid Queen – "just accept what is and be grateful."

My wife and I were honored to be invited to attend the *bedoyo ketawang* dance to honor the cosmic marriage between Senopati and Ratu Kidul.

It was originally performed as a six-hour marathon, all the better to put the dancers and audience into a trance-like state. Today, the occasional ringing of guests' cell phones reminds us that we live in a faster world, and the dance has been shortened to 90 minutes. Nevertheless, the atmosphere is reminiscent of a gaudy, precious, but down-at-the-heels

19th century operetta, but it is still otherwordly, with spirits in the air, as the special gamelan orchestra *pings* and *glongs* a deliberate beat that accompanies a high-pitched female singer.

In the wrong frame of mind, the *bedoyo ketawang* can be tedious, but when I remembered a friend's advice to "switch mode," it became considerably more entrancing and elegant. Just as western Baroque music has been shown to induce relaxation (and learning) by reducing a person's heart rate and decreasing blood pressure, I have the impression that the *bedoyo ketawang* music, played on sacred gongs and xylophones used only on this occasion, alters our consciousness. Let's call it a Kanjeng Ratu Kidul-enhanced altered state.

We saw nine young women (virgins, according to palace protocol) wearing sacred dark blue and white batik sarongs, colors that symbolize the contrasts of earth and ocean, light and darkness, royalty and commoner. They wore hair extensions pulled back in *chignons* entwined with golden filigree and jasmine garlands. They had been rehearsing for weeks, and were forbidden to dance if they were menstruating.

During the reception that followed the dance, a man named Ki Radu Kusumodiningrat asked if I wanted to "speak with Kanjeng Ratu Kidul." I wasn't too sure what he meant but said yes anyway.

Ki Radu Kusumodiningrat, a relative of the susuhunan, is a traditional healer. His colleague, Raden Ayu Retno Handayati, the purported medium who was going to channel the Mermaid Queen, was also a distant relative; she works as an acupuncturist and massage therapist. We stopped at a market to buy fruit, candles, and incense, then went back to our hotel for the séance. The doorman busted us for the pungent-smelling durian, and out of respect for the no-smoking signs in the room, we canceled the incense, but the medium, Raden Ayu Retno Handayati, wasn't perturbed. She put on her veil and intoned an Arabic blessing. Her voice shifted to the timbre of that of a young woman and she asked our names. We suspended belief and imagined we were speaking with the Mermaid Queen herself.

We asked her about her love affair with Senopati, and in return got romantic platitudes, sort of Javanese Hallmark card sentiments.

"Were you present just now at the *bedoyo ketawang?*"

Raden Ayu Retno Handayati, perhaps channeling Kanjeng Ratu Kidul, smiled and answered enigmatically, "I'm always present for the sultan."

We saw she was getting tired, but just before the channeling ended, the Mermaid Queen offered me personal support and invited me on a date, Javanese Mermaid-Queen-style. "Just go to the southern coast," she said, "call my name, stamp your foot three times, and I will be there for you."

I am intrigued by the possibility that Kanjeng Ratu Kidul was present at the dance, and put the question to one of the *bedoyo ketawang* dancers. Wuri, 23, is a soft-spoken English teacher at a local elementary school in Solo, who didn't find the question strange. "Yes, I had a feeling Ratu Kidul was there. One time I made a mistake in my movement and I felt her correcting me."

Another dancer, Putri, 21, acknowledged that toward the end of the performance she felt a current of air, as if Kanjeng Ratu Kidul was "going to the sultan."

The morning after the *bedoyo ketawang*, we ran into one of the susuhunan's close relatives, who was staying at the same hotel as us. Over croissants we asked the elegantly dressed woman about the previous day's performance and whether she thought that Kanjeng Ratu Kidul had appeared.

"Absolutely," she said. Her eyes started to get misty and a dreamy look, wonderful to see in a woman of a certain age, came over her face. "There was a rush of cool air. That was the queen, going to the king."

Again, I tried to ask a Cartesian question in a polite way.

"What did you make of all this?"

In a wistful voice, perhaps more suited to a love-struck school girl, she answered, "It's a love affair for the ages."

In the mid-1980s I interviewed Sultan Hamengku Buwono IX of Yogyakarta about his relationship with Kanjeng Ratu Kidul. The late sultan was a key figure in modern Indonesia's history since he played a vital diplomatic role during the Japanese occupation in WWII, helping to lead the fight for independence from the Dutch.

His public encounter with Kanjeng Ratu Kidul took place every June 21, when the sultan trekked to the dangerous surf on the slate-gray southern coast of Java. There he offered a full set of women's clothing and his own nail and hair clippings to pay homage.

In 1984 I was granted an audience in his souvenir-filled Jakarta office. There was one question I wanted to ask him and tried to phrase it in a refined Javanese manner. How was it that a man as pragmatic and cosmopolitan as the sultan – he had been vice-president of Indonesia and had also held various ministerial posts – could pay homage every year to a mermaid queen?

Instead of answering directly, Sultan Hamengku Buwono IX offered me sweet tea and a story. "One night during the Dutch occupation of Yogyakarta, while my family was living in the *kraton* [palace], we heard soldiers moving noisily about, as if wearing armour. It is said they were the soldiers of Ratu Kidul protecting the *kraton*." I pressed him for details. "There was no one in the *kraton* except our family and staff," he said matter-of-factly. "But we all heard the soldiers' drums."

I was more than a little sceptical of this, as well as of several other tales he told, of Kanjeng Ratu Kidul's timely interventions that changed the course of Indonesia's history. The sultan didn't quote Shakespeare, but he might as well have. He gave me the Javanese equivalent of "There are more things in heaven and earth, Horatio, than are dreamt of in your philosophy." He concluded: "When I was four years old I was already living with a Dutch family, so my brain is in some ways a Western brain. But many things happen which can't be explained in a logical way."

I must have looked bewildered.

The sultan then told me not to get too caught up in a Cartesian view of the world. "You're asking a Western question, expecting a Western answer," he admonished. "You either accept it or you don't."

There is much magic in the air throughout Java. Accept it or not. One man's myth-enrobed fantasy is another man's hard-nosed reality. In the rainbow-hued world of shifting Javanese cosmology, reality can be as ethereal as a wisp; like religion, like a miracle, like love, you believe it. Or not.

In October 2010 Mount Merapi erupted, spewing ash and lava and poison gas that killed 353 people and displaced 350,000. Javanese pundits attribute the eruption to Kanjeng Ratu Kidul's irritation with, as one old man told me, "Indonesia's impure behavior." But a satellite photograph of the Merapi Golf Course shortly after the eruptions showed that once again the course had been spared — lava covered one hole and damaged parts of five holes; the rest of the course, which by rights should have been obliterated, was undamaged and playable.

# THE FLYING PHALLUS AND THE MONSTER DRIVE

Seeking protection and the long ball
on the golf trail in Bhutan.

## THIMPHU, Bhutan

THE COUNTRY THAT OWNS THE TRADEMARK TO "Gross National Happiness" is also home to a minor, but nevertheless irritating cause of despair – the deepest bunker I've seen on a golf course.

Near the second green on the Royal Thimphu Golf Course, I faced a sand shot that had to clear the bunker's front face, as high as a pro basketball center. I needed Lama Drukpa Kunley's assistance.

More to the point, I needed the assistance of Lama Drukpa Kunley's symbolic phallus.

Phalluses – sometimes simple and stylized, often ornate and anatomically correct – adorn many houses in Bhutan. And these phalluses must do a good job since Bhutan is famously pacifist, the people are largely content, and the Switzerlandsized landlocked kingdom is relatively free of the trouble-some domestic dramas that afflict other Asian countries.

After the golf, while on a trek along the Nabji-Korphu Trail in the Jigme-Singye Wangchuck National Park, I decided to acquire a phallus-totem from Karma, a village artist in central Bhutan.

"I can make you a new phallus, no problem," Karma assured me.

"But we're leaving in the morning."

"Trust me."

Most of the holes of Royal Thimphu have a view of the 17th-century Tashichho Dzong, a massive, fairy-tale-like construction that, like the other dzongs in the country, serves as monastery, government headquarters, fort, temple, and cultural center.

On the downhill 5th hole, I was faced with a blind tee-shot. My caddie Rinchen, 16, told me to aim my drive toward the king's office on the top floor of the distant dzong.

The medieval dzong was the setting for the 2008 coronation of Jigme Khesar Namgyel Wangchuck as Bhutan's fifth king (practical Bhutanese refer to the young new monarch as K5, to distinguish him from his still very active father, King Jigme Singye Wangchuck, known as K4). The event, with full Himalayan pomp and circumstance, represented two rare events in world history. The first is that the much-loved and very healthy K4 abdicated in favor of his son. The second was that the king relinquished much of his power and initiated a democratic government. The Bhutanese were perplexed. We love our king, they said, and we trust his judgment. Why change a good thing?

It is a truism that Bhutan is doing its best to maintain its culture in a rapidly changing world – when the capital Thimphu got its first traffic light, the king ordered it dismantled because it didn't feel sufficiently Bhutanese.

And Bhutan is sandwiched between two big, annoying neighbors: India to the south and China to the north.

Tourism was discouraged in Bhutan until 1974, and it wasn't until 1999 that Bhutan got television and the Internet.

Golf, however, came earlier, in the early 1970s. The pioneers were an Indian army officer and Paljor Dorji, a cousin of K4. According to Rick Lipsey, an American journalist who became Royal Thimphu's first golf pro and who started the Bhutan Youth Golf Association, the Tashichho Dzong (literally "the fortress of auspicious doctrine") "was surrounded by putrid rice paddies. The Indian army officer told King Jigme Singye Wangchuck that he could turn the glop into a manicured lawn by building a golf course. The king was unfamiliar with golf, but he liked the idea of a green oasis, and the course opened a few years later."

K4, in fact became a competent golfer; writer John Barton recalls that the name at the top of the handicap sheet at Royal Thimphu Golf Course is "one member whose [handicap] number is 13.2. His name is displayed simply as 'His Majesty.'"

According to the king's cousin, Paljor Dorji, or Benji as he prefers to be known, K4 only plays once or twice a year. "He likes to play fast and everybody else on the course moves out of his way to let him pass. So he feels he's disturbing them."

Acquiring a phallus seemed to be a practical and economical form of Asian homeowners' insurance. Of course there was no guarantee that the wooden phallus, once imported to Thailand, would have the same anti-demon properties that it provides in this landlocked, traditional country, but I figured it was worth a ten-dollar investment.

Mind you, I already had an ample dose of good luck.

Only a handful of trekkers are allowed to pitch their tents at each of the Jigme Singye Wangchuck National Park's six campsites and we virtually had the area to ourselves. I spent hours sitting on a rock next to a river, watching deep-blue kingfishers dart into the clear mountain water. What good fortune to be virtually alone in one of Asia's most interesting and beautiful protected areas.

But if a little good luck is nice, then surely lots of phallus-inspired good luck and protection would be even better.

The 9-hole Royal Thimphu Golf Course is one of seven courses in the country, and the only one open to the public. It is the home of the annual Yak Open, with "yak parts as prizes."

A 16th-century brick chorten, a distinctive and common Tibetan Buddhist monument, sits just behind the third tee. The size of a small cabin, the building is white-washed with a distinctive red horizontal stripe and a slate roof. In less tumultuous, pre-golf times, merit-makers would leave offerings of jade, silver, and turquoise for the Buddhist tantric spirits. But the chorten is empty now; thieves stole the easy pickings. They were caught, though, and languish in prison.

Rick Lipsey writes how this particular chorten "has been regaining its devotional importance ... The golfers dream about it. They lustily stare at it ... But it's not Lord Buddha whom the Bhutanese golfers think about when they look at the chorten. It's Lord Long Ball." The 2nd and 3rd holes at Royal Thimphu are parallel, and from the second tee, a golfer takes clear aim at the chorten, some 460 meters (500 yards) distant. Like most spiritual quests, the grail of reaching the chorten with a decade-old driver and a scratched Top-Flite is likely to remain out of reach for most pilgrims. Nevertheless, Bhutan's golfers, like most pilgrims, relentlessly seek and flail in search of the unattainable.

It seems the spiritual world and the secular realities are rarely far apart in modern-day Bhutan.

Throughout Asia, folks rely on cosmic bodyguards that might come in the form of mystical tattoos, amulets, incantations, and making of merit.

The Bhutanese choose the male reproductive organ to ensure that a home is free from evil spirits and slander.

These phallus images, called *po* in Dzonghka, Bhutan's national language, are sometimes painted on the outside walls of Bhutanese houses, sometimes carved from wood and hung from the eaves of their sturdy stone and timber dwellings. Dasho Karma Ura, head of the Center for Bhutan Studies, describes these phalluses as "exuberant and gifted penises, always slightly askew and sometimes frothy."

The man who generally gets credited with popularizing the good-luck-phallus craze was a 15th- to 16th-century Buddhist yogi named Lama Drukpa Kunley. He was to phallus popularity what Brigitte Bardot was to the bikini.

Unlike the gentle and placid approach of mainstream Buddhist missionaries, Drukpa Kunley proselytized through anarchy, shock, and awe. He believed that only by spotlighting the absurdity of all fixed, man-made rules, and by forcing the student to abandon all ideas of predictability and emotional security, could people become wise enough to understand the "crazy wisdom" of Buddhist enlightenment.

Drukpa Kunley, *enfant terrible* of Buddhist missionaries, seducer of women (including his own mother, but it was for her own good, he argued), famously subdued the female demons of Bhutan with his "flaming thunderbolt." He exemplified the tantric belief that carnal relations can be the gateway to enlightenment, and was not hesitant to enlighten as many women as possible.

In many countries an urban golf course is an oasis of green amidst urban gray. However, the scenery from every hole of Royal Thimphu is of hills enrobed with untrammeled forests, a sea of green that surrounds the small Bhutanese capital.

But what are unnatural and unpleasant are the greenside water hazards — man-made concrete ponds that resemble giant, algae-clogged, disused swimming pools.

As we were finishing breakfast the following morning, Karma, the village artist, strolled into our camp with what appeared to be a colorful model airplane.

On closer examination we saw that he had carved a pink-painted phallus as long as my forearm. To the business end of the phallus, Karma had added a strip of faded yellow cloth, perhaps an homage to the ubiquitous prayer flags found throughout the country, but more likely representing Anti-Demon Ejaculate. He had also carved a wooden sword, which he nailed at right angles to the phallus, giving the object the approximate look of a handmade, not-quite-completed B-52. Our friend and trekking guide Tashi Namgay explained that while the phallus provides protection, the wooden sword "cuts through ignorance, the first step toward wisdom."

My French wife dubbed it the "Flying Zizi," using the French slang for the male member.

We took our Flying Zizi to the simple village temple, set in the middle of a paddy field. We quickly located Dorji, a lay monk who doubled as the shrine's caretaker. He didn't flinch as we asked him to bless the object.

While Bhutan's neighbors are experiencing a golf boom, Bhutan plods along in its own quiet way. Only Royal Thimphu is open to foreign visitors. Other courses in the country are the par-32 9-hole Wangdi Military Base Course with sand greens, the course at India House with eight greens and six fairways, and the king's private layout on his property in Punhaka. Another three courses, located on military bases, range from four to eight holes.

I asked our friend Tashi Namgay, "Will our wooden phallus work against all demons?"

"Actually, the really tough demons require something stronger," Tashi replied, his unwavering patience for our ridiculous questions tempered now with a hint of good-natured sarcasm.

"An extra large phallus, perhaps?"

"No, just the opposite. Naked dancing monks."

In reply to our perplexed looks, Tashi explained that this tiny village of Nabji, a day's walk from the nearest road, was the epicenter for other significant phallus-phenomena.

To simplify a complex legend, in centuries past a group

of devotees in Nabji had been trying to build a temple. Each day they would labor in the warm sun, and each night, as the workers slept, the mischievous anti-religious demons would tear down the holy structure. Finally, a monk named Dorje Lingpa led a nocturnal dance of naked men in order to distract the demons. The strategy worked, and eventually, following days of hot work and nights of cold dancing (and, one assumes, diminished zizis), the temple was built.

And the deepest bunker in the world? I knocked the ball out backwards, giving me an easy chip to the green. Sometimes golf shots, like spiritual quests, don't need to be tackled head-on.

On our return to Thailand, in May 2010, the people of Bangkok were tensing for a battle between rival Red Shirts and Yellow Shirts. A military intervention seemed certain, and just a few blocks away, armed soldiers were gathering for a final showdown with the implacable demonstrators.

We carefully unpacked our Flying Zizi and hung it in our Thai garden. "This will work in Bangkok?" I had asked Karma when we had purchased the talisman a few weeks earlier.

That kind of question may have been a touch too abstract for Karma, a village boy who had never even been to the Bhutanese capital of Thimpu. But the shrug he gave us seemed to say, "can't hurt."

And he was right. While central Bangkok burned, life on our little *soi* continued relatively undisturbed. The noodle vendor in front of our house stayed open, as did the grilled chicken lady, the vegetable seller, and the motorcycle taxi guys. The cat slept peacefully. I'm not too sure that the sword helped us to cut through ignorance to achieve wisdom, but I'm pretty certain that at least the phallus-fearing demons went elsewhere.

# MOVE OVER SCOTLAND; CHINA INVENTED GOLF

And it's coming home to the Middle Kingdom.

————————

## HONG KONG,
## On the outskirts of the Middle Kingdom

THE SCOTS NEVER KNEW WHAT HIT THEM.

Everyone knows that the sturdy Scots invented golf. After all, the first written record about golf comes from 1457, when King James II banned the game because his subjects preferred it to archery practice, which made golf a threat to national security.

But now the Middle Kingdom has staked a claim. Academics from China, which has famously given the world gunpowder, spaghetti, and paper, not to mention the compass, the umbrella, and the rudder, and which claims that its sailors discovered America decades before Columbus, assert that golf is in fact a Chinese game.

The evidence comes from a Ming dynasty scroll exhibited in a 2006 exhibit at the Hong Kong Heritage Museum. Titled "The Autumn Banquet," the painting, which has been dated as early as 1368, shows a well-coifed Chinese gentleman swinging a stick that could be a golf club at a small sphere that resembles a golf ball, toward what clearly is a hole in the ground in the midst of what just might be a green.

Even more troubling for the Scots (not to mention the French, the Dutch, the Belgians, and even the Laotians who have staked claims to this venerable game) is a reproduction, also shown in the Hong Kong exhibition, of a Yuan dynasty (1271–1368) mural showing courtiers wielding golf-like sticks. The painting is accompanied by a book *Wan Jing*, or *Manual of the Ball Game*, which was published in 1282 and provides rules for a game that doesn't seem that far from our contemporary pastime.

According to Professor Ling Hongling of Lanzhou University, an even earlier Song Dynasty (960–1279) book called the *Dongxuan Records* describes a game called *chiuwan* – literally "hit-ball." It was played with ten different gold- and jade-encrusted clubs, including a flat-surfaced *cuanbang* – equivalent to a modern-day driver, and a *shaobang*, similar to a 3-wood. Giving the golf-proud Scots no quarter, Ling adds that the Chinese book refers to a prominent Chinese magistrate of the Nantang era (937–975) who instructed his daughter "to dig holes in the ground so that he might drive a ball into them with a purposely crafted stick."

Regardless of the veracity of these claims, it was clearly the Europeans, particularly the British, who brought golf back to Asia.

The expatriate Brits developed Asia's first golf course in 1826 – Royal Calcutta in India – and British planters subsequently built courses near their estates in Peninsular Malaysia and Burma.

Rana aristocrats returning from visits to Scotland brought golf to Nepal as early as 1829, when the Royal Nepal Golf Course was built, and British merchants built Sri Lanka's first course, the Royal Colombo Golf Course, in 1879.

The Dutch, too, make a claim to have invented golf. As early as the 13th century, they played a hole-less game called *colfe*. The chronicler of a 1596 Dutch expedition led by Willem Barentsz (after whom the Barents Sea, north of Norway and Russia, is named) wrote that when the crew was forced to spend the winter in the Arctic (the first overwintering in that harsh region ever attempted by European explorers), the earnest crew "made a staffe to plaie at colfe, thereby to stretch our Jointes ... and make them nymble." Writer David Roberts explains that contemporary etchings, one of them by Rembrandt, "show spheroids the size of croquet balls and clubs that look more like field hockey sticks than 3-woods. In the etchings there is nary a pin or cup in sight."

Regardless of whether *colfe* was a direct forerunner to modern-day golf, the Dutch had a hand in promoting golf in Asia, establishing Indonesia's first course, in 1872. This was the Batavia Golf Club, now the Jakarta Golf Club (generally referred to as Rawamangun), a favorite early- morning sporting venue for high-ranking government officials.

Foreign invention or not, golf in Asia has taken off higher than a kite (another Chinese invention) throughout Asia, and in particular in China itself.

As one pundit exclaimed, in China the glories of the Ming Dynasty might be giving way to the Ping Dynasty. Back in 1982, just three years after China's "reform and opening up" policy, Arnold Palmer designed the mainland's first modern golf course. The number of courses grew from 20 in 1994 to some 200 in 2004, when government officials put a moratorium on new course development due to environmental-impact concerns. This suspension was heartily ignored, and the country now has more than 600 courses; China currently ranks fifth in the world and second in Asia (tied with South Korea and Thailand) in terms of the number of courses.

Gary Player, one of the most successful professional golfers and a noted golf course architect in his own right, says, "My insight is that Asians may have more passion for golf than any other people in the world." Player, who has designed more than 30 courses in Asia, says that "the growth potential is staggering."

This boom doesn't mean that all the golf courses make money.

The Japan Golf Membership Prices Index (the fact that such an economic index exists speaks volumes about how entrenched golf is in that country), which monitors joining fees in some 500 golf clubs nationwide, has fallen below its starting level in 1982, after rising nearly 700 percent at its peak in 1990. Similarly, the Singapore Business Times Golf Index, which tracks membership values in seven clubs, is down more than a third from its highest point in 1994.

Sam Ng, a reporter at Asia Times Online says that "almost half of China's more than 200 courses are running a deficit."

In Thailand, where many golf clubs are struggling to just pay their debts, Les Walsh, of Golfworks Thailand, which organizes corporate golfing events and tours, says, "only about five percent [of the clubs] are profitable." But Robin Moyer, publisher of Golfing Asia Publications in Hong Kong is more bullish, saying that "the Asian golf boom is here to stay."

What makes the game so appealing?

Guy Goh, a Singaporean who started *Golf Vacations* magazine, feels that golf is still a growing industry. He suggests that "with urbanization and increased stress, the affluent in Asia need to get closer to nature, and a golf course, with its trees and water hazards, is a perfect environment in which to relax."

Dudi Boedhihartono, a Thailand-based Indonesian businessman and self-confessed golf junkie, attributes the Asian golf boom in part to the popularity of Tiger Woods, who is half-Thai, and to the global success of Asian golfers. But there are other reasons, he argues, citing "it's high profile, a good place to seal business deals, and suits itself to gambling." Ultimately, though, he says that "today's Asian golfers play golf simply because they love the game."

Both Goh and Boedhihartono imply that money aside, golf in and of itself is fun, challenging, and surprising – sometimes even otherworldly. Which leads to one final candidate for the "inventor" of golf. Some people suggest we should venture beyond the Middle Kingdom and look toward Middle Earth. In *The Hobbit* it is said that Bullroarer Took invented the game of golf when he knocked a goblin's head down a hole.

# FIRE AND FURY MIGHT HAVE TO WAIT FOR THE NEXT LIFETIME

The Indian Army controls the world's highest golf course, bringing a breathtaking set of challenges.

———◆◆◆———

## LADAKH, India

I THOUGHT IT MIGHT BE THE ALTITUDE THAT WOULD get to me, but it turned out to be military bureaucracy.

Since my first visit in 1979, I had wanted to play golf in Ladakh, an isolated corner of northern India that forms part of the high-altitude Tibetan plateau. I wasn't particularly interested in golf during that visit thirty years earlier, but I nevertheless vividly remembered the sight of black "greens" sitting amidst an ochre-colored wasteland. The sight appealed to my sense of the ridiculous. What was a golf course doing up there in a land of Tibetan monks, yaks, and oxygen-deficient atmosphere?

But the altitude – where climbing a flight of stairs felt to me like Hillary's and Tenzing's struggle to the summit of Everest, turned out to be a non-factor. I had underestimated that classic oxymoron – military intelligence.

Over the years I got the golf bug, and when I visited India's capital, New Delhi, in 2006 on business, I made some calls to see what it would take to play in Ladakh.

"Yes, there is a course," a well-placed friend, himself a retired officer, advised. "But it's military. Closed to the public."

"I'm not the public. I'm a journalist."

"I'll see what I can do."

My friend put me in touch with another military friend, a colonel based in Ladakh, who had some influence.

While I was still in Delhi, I called him and said, "I'll be in Ladakh tomorrow. Can I see you?"

The next morning I arrived on the dawn flight to Ladakh's capital, Leh, to discover that my cell phone didn't work. I eventually found a phone in my hotel (charmingly named The Yak Tail) and called the colonel, whom I hoped would be my savior.

"What? You're in Leh? I say, bad planning. I'm in Delhi for a meeting," he said, once again showing how two people can be separated by a common language. "Not good at all. I need to get your passport, and get permission, and ..."

So I went directly to the course, spoke to the soldier in charge, and wrote a note to an even more senior officer based locally, who I was told had the power to grant me access.

In the meantime I strolled around the course, which lies just a drive and 5-iron from a street of shops.

Next to the first tee, named Sher Shah Suri after the 15th-century Moghul "Lion King," is a signboard reading: "Built 1967 as Trishul Golf Course, renamed Fire and Fury in 1999. 18 holes, 6,612 meters, par 72." Nothing about restricted access.

I stood on the elevated tee box, a room-sized construction rising about a meter off the ground. It was covered with dried mud, and in the center was a pizza-sized patch of scraggly grass, a golf course equivalent of Yasser Arafat's three-day stubble. Those few blades were about the only green found anywhere on the course. I later learned that most golfers carry their own little mats with them to use on the tees.

Just next to the first tee was the green for the 10th hole, dubbed "10 Downing Street." It wasn't too hard to see that the course was maintained by the Army Corps of Engineers – this particular green was perfectly square, and the bunker next to it was perfectly rectangular.

Actually the green wasn't green. It was black. I studied the substance – motor oil mixed with sand. A ball rolled more or less true, but slowly.

I walked around the course. In one section several gardeners were planting hundreds of willow trees to provide ... I'm not too sure what the purpose was. A golfing challenge? A touch of green? A practical horticultural exercise in drip irrigation?

Ladakh is mostly a high altitude desert, and even though the region had a snowy winter, during my early-spring visit, the golf course appeared lunar and severe – brown and unwelcoming. It's set in a bowl, about three kilometers long and one kilometer wide, with stunning views of the Khardang Mountains. I could see the road winding up to the Khardang-la pass, which at 5,603 meters is the world's highest motorable road.

This is high country, populated by ethnic Tibetans who sometimes appear closer to the secrets of the cosmos than flat-dwellers.

Is Fire and Fury, at 3,445 meters (11,300 feet), the world's highest golf course?

The Tuctu Golf Club in Peru, high in the Andes at 4,335 meters (14,200 feet), once held the record, but it was abandoned over a decade ago and is now, according to one report, an unplayable mass of bush and vegetation.

With Tuctu out of action, Ladakh's Fire and Fury is certainly the highest 18-hole golf course in the world. Next comes La Paz Golf Club in Bolivia, at 3,292 meters (10,800 feet), which can stake a claim to be the highest *grass* course in the world.

By comparison, the highest United States courses are non-contenders in the nosebleed sweepstakes. Mount Massive, a 9-hole course in Leadville, Colorado, claims to be the highest course in North America at 9,690 feet (2,950 meters), but the highest 18-hole course is Copper Creek Golf Club at Copper Mountain, also in Colorado. Its clubhouse, the location where official altitude is determined, is at 9,500 feet (2,895 meters), but portions of the course climb to 9,700 feet (2,956 meters).

I eventually met some high-ranking officers at the military barracks in Leh. Their responses were similar: "Too bad you're here for such a short time, we'd love to play with you but you have to get an intelligence clearance."

"But it's a golf course," I argued.

"Yes, but it's also a military training area."

Ladakh occupies a strategic position – the territory is scrunched between perennial enemies Pakistan (the countries have fought three bitter wars since 1947) and China (a border war in 1962), making it a geopolitical hotspot. I saw that the military commanders weren't going to bend to make a middle-aged American writer happy.

So I pursued an alternative path and consulted Venerable Nawang Luto, a monk at the nearby Spituk monastery, whom I had befriended in 1979.

Although thirty years had passed he said he remembered

me (he either has a fine memory or is a skilled diplomat). He listened to my tale and, with the wisdom of decades of Tibetan meditation behind him, basically said, "I can pray for your soul but the army is out of my control."

Nevertheless, I'm optimistic that if I return to Ladakh I will be granted permission to play Fire and Fury. I've already got my talisman – an electric blue golf cap bearing the Fire and Fury logo. Not taking any chances, I also acquired a Tibetan prayer wheel that sends entreaties toward the heavens. So even if I don't get to play the course in this lifetime, I can perhaps take solace in the philosophy of my monk friend Nawang Luto. Existence is a cycle, and if things don't work out in this life, there will always be another opportunity in another lifetime to play the gravel course at Fire and Fury. In the meantime, I'm breathing deeply and practicing my shots off dirt.

# GOLF: AN ANTIDOTE TO WAR AND HARDSHIP

Could golf in Iran help people love one another?

———◦×◦———

## TEHRAN, Iran

AND ALL ALONG I HAD THOUGHT GOLF WAS A CAUSE of anxiety.

"No, just the opposite. Golf *relieves* stress," Eisa Eshagi, president of the Iranian Golf Federation, said. "And that's what we need, since we're a nation that has suffered wars and hardships."

Few in the West would immediately think of Iran as a beleaguered nation. But of course it's all about perspective. Iran lost some 600,000 people during the 1980–1988 war with Iraq, and in 2003 a huge earthquake killed at least 15,000 people near the ancient city of Bam.

Iranians have other reasons to feel defensive these days. After all, George W. Bush has damned the country as part of the "axis of evil," and the U.S. State Departmen, regularly reminds us of Iran's close relationships with Libya, Syria, and North Korea, telling Americans that Iran is secretly building nuclear weapons, supporting insurgents in Iraq, and channeling aid to terrorist group Hezbollah.

Nevertheless, Iran has been undergoing a halting process

of reform, encouraged by diplomatic engagement and trade with European states – and to a lesser extent with the United States.

So, as an American, and as a golfer, I went to Tehran with personal and geopolitical curiosity.

Wherever I went in this polluted city of 11 million, where drivers seem to practice for bumper car tournaments and where upper-class head-scarved women push the envelope to see how much fashion style they can get away with without getting busted by the morality police, I was met with consistent courtesy and often with warmth – many Iranians have family and friends in the States. Once again I was reminded that it's essential to separate the posturing of respective governments from the attitudes of ordinary people.

I traveled to Iran as part of my job with the International Osteoporosis Foundation – disease obviously respects no political frontiers.

But, having an afternoon free after consulting with our member society and meeting the former president, Ayatollah Rafsanjani, to seek his support of osteoporosis-education activities, I drove to the north of the city to play at the country's only grass golf course, Enghelab.

I was intrigued by the idea of playing what is arguably the ultimate "Western" (and therefore "morally corrupt") sport in a country effectively run by conservative mullahs.

And I had never played on a 13-hole course. Enghelab, which means "revolution" in Farsi, lost five of its holes in 1992 when the military confiscated the land for housing and facilities.

In 1999 Bob Cullen, writing in *Golf Digest*, described a course "inexorably being reclaimed by desert weeds," with bushes two meters high in front of the tee, and with fuel tanks, freshly dug ditches, and "a pile of construction rubble" creating a challenging series of fairway obstacles.

My, what a difference five years makes.

Today, Iranian authorities obviously think that sports are perfectly compatible with the nation's goals.

The Enghelab course is set within the vast Enghelab Sports Complex, with good facilities for gymnastics, wrestling, horse riding, tennis, and swimming (with separate men's and women's pools).

Cullen had written that the Revolutionary Guards had confiscated the land of the missing five holes, and the fear of the quasi-military zealots still pervaded the area.

Enroute to Enghelab my taxi passed the outer fence of the golf course, and I asked the driver to stop so I could take a photo of the buildings that were constructed on previous golf course land.

"No, no, you can't take pictures here," the driver said. "Military."

So I put my camera away and drove to the new offices of the Iranian Golf Federation where Eisa Eshagi, who had been on the job just three weeks, told me of his ambitious goal to popularize golf in the Islamic Republic, with plans to build driving ranges, enter players in the 2006 Asian championships in Qatar, establish a website, and invite the public to try the game during golf introduction days.

Eshagi, 33, a relative newcomer to the game, explained, "I used to think golf was for old people, but it's very exciting. And Iranians like new sports."

"And golf is politically correct?" I asked, remembering how Iran's government politicizes sports (Iran's Arash Miresmaeili, a world judo champion, refused to compete against an Israeli in the 2004 Athens Olympics, citing "sympathy with the struggling Palestinian people.").

"Sure."

"And women can play?"

"Why not? The vice-president of the Iranian Golf Federation is a woman."

I saw that his third-floor office had a lovely view of the

golf course, including the (rather benign-looking) military constructions that had usurped five holes of the course. Could I take a photo from his balcony? "Be my guest," he replied.

Earlier, I had corresponded with Simon Dicksee, a British instructor who had been sent to Tehran by the PGA of Europe to coach Iranian golfers. Dicksee noted that two golfers had "international potential." I was hoping to meet one of the promising golfers, Hasan Karimian, who doubles as the Enghelab pro. He is also the Iranian national champ, which arguably makes him the 13-hole champion of the world.

Even from a distance I could pick out Karimian – like many club pros, he had the infuriating ability to bounce a ball on his pitching wedge and then hit the golf ball baseball style, just like Tiger does in those commercials.

It was late afternoon and about a dozen people were on the practice range, including a handful of young women. So Eshagi was right – golf *is* a sport that men and women can play together. The lady golfers wore the customary head coverings and robes, but perched jauntily on one lady's head, on top of the head scarf, was a Nike baseball cap.

Karimian, 27, had half an hour before his next lesson and agreed to play a couple of holes with me and another member of the club, one of a hundred golfers who pay about $4 a round, to play Enghelab (foreigners have to fork out about $50 per round).

He loaned me a decent set of clubs – clones of a well-known brand. We started on the 10th. The fairway was wide and open and I hit a good drive.

"Where's the green?" I asked Hasan.

"Hit a 9-iron to just in front of that line of trees," he instructed.

I did and still couldn't see the green through the trees.

"Can't you see the flag?" he asked. The trees bordered a

hidden stream that crossed immediately in front of the green. I had maybe 30 yards to clear two-story-tall trees and immediately drop the ball down onto the green. I pitched high enough, but long. No problem, though, there was plenty of landing area. I chipped back and two-putted. Double bogey six.

"What do you say when you miss an easy putt?"

Karimian indicated a common four-letter English expletive beginning with "F."

"But in Farsi?"

"Same word."

I had done my homework, though. An Iranian expatriate friend in Geneva had taught me several colorful Farsi expressions. I muttered one of them under my breath. (I don't know much Farsi, but it seems like one of those guttural languages – Dutch, Cantonese, Danish, Mongolian also come to mind – that lend themselves to swearing.)

The course was in surprisingly good shape. Sure, the tee boxes were often an uneven combination of heavy grass and bare earth, and the fairways were irregularly mowed and often overgrown, and okay, the greens were either rock hard or swamp-like from overzealous hand watering, but it was a functioning golf course with plenty of challenges.

Karimian left to give a lesson, and I continued with Bahram, a retired engineer whose son lives in California. I was pleased to see that the threesome in front of us was made up of two men and a woman.

On the 13th hole (which doubles as the fourth), I hit a good drive, then pitched to the green. The ball rolled toward the pin and, about two yards from the hole, it disappeared. As I approached the green I saw the reason – smack in the middle of the green was a sprinkler head, set to a depth of about a foot, about as big as the medium-sized pizza I had eaten earlier that day at Boff Fast Food restaurant. Bahram wasn't sure about the ruling, but I gave myself a free drop on the green.

The last hole at Enghelab has a narrow fairway, dogleg left, heading toward the Elburz mountains, as burnt-out and sere as the sexless cloaks that women are forced to wear in public. I thought of Eisa Eshaghi's philosophy. *Golf reduces stress.* What if he's right? I slowed my breathing and nailed the drive, and then nailed an 8-iron to the green, missing the sprinkler head. My putt was just short. No stress. No colorful language. Tap-in par. Maybe Eisa Eshagi has something there.

# GOLF THAT GOES BUMP IN THE NIGHT

Nat spirits, hermit monks, and a farm boy who plays off eight make Mount Popa Golf Course an otherworldly experience.

———

## MOUNT POPA, Myanmar

THERE IS STRANGE MAGIC IN THE AIR.

For a start, U Moe Ting, my caddie at this unprepossessing course in central Myanmar, tells me to "hit toward the trees."

There is no fairway in sight, just an ox cart trundling in the brush along the spot where my drive would probably land. But never mind – farm boy U Moe Ting plays off eight, using golf clubs that resemble gardening tools, so who was I to challenge his judgment?

And he was right. I hit my drive on the second hole and the ball landed in a hidden flat patch that revealed an opening to the previously camouflaged dogleg. Local knowledge helps, especially when the *nats* are out and about.

*Nats* are the mystical and mischievous souls of legendary people (who seem to have died mostly horrible deaths) and hold dominion over a place, person, or field of experience. In predominantly Buddhist Myanmar, *nats* take on the role of elves, leprechauns, Santa Claus, and kitchen gods. Lord Buddha takes care of the big things – life, death, and salvation – but *nats*, a form of animistic spirit-guardians, are where the spiritual rubber meets the road, the cosmic adjudicators of school exams and teenage romance, business success and lottery tickets.

And Mount Popa, sometimes described as the Mount Olympus of Myanmar, is *nat* Ground-Zero. Located some 50 kilometers southeast of Bagan, this is among Myanmar's spaciest locations. Besides the ubiquitous *nat*-spirits, Mount Popa is home to snake charmers who control when the monsoons will arrive, a hermit cave-dwelling monk, a jungle path with so many butterflies that I felt like I was in a lepidoptera-ticker tape parade, and a conjurer who smashed my watch with a hammer and, for a small fee, put it back together again.

A few days after my golf game, I trekked an hour up a butterfly-enhanced forest path on Mount Popa, arguably the most mystical hill in this most mystical of countries, to visit a hermit monk named Venerable U Sumana.

Hesitantly, I approached the cave and saw a young monk preparing a fire. I asked if I was disturbing him. Popping in unannounced suddenly seemed like a stupid idea – the last thing I wanted to do was get in the way of his accumulation of karma points. Nevertheless, for a recluse, U Sumana was remarkably outgoing. He had finished his morning prayers, he explained, and invited me to sit on the ledge and chat.

Several years earlier, U Sumana had taken over the cave that had been the home of U Jermani, a legendary monk who meditated in this damp, isolated ledge for fifty years. U Sumana had few possessions, few clothes, and his diet consisted of a handful of rice and some vegetables. To me such isolation, deprivation, and rigor would be purgatory. I like my diversions too much – Beethoven, a fine wine, golf, pizza, and the company of friends. U Sumana, though, had a different view of his adopted home. "It's shady and cool. It's easy to get water. I'm in the middle of nature and there's no one around to distract me from my prayers." He had bright eyes and an easy smile. He explained he had seen this cave in a dream and journeyed here from distant Mon state.

My rational, Cartesian mind was racing. "But what do you do all day?" I asked.

U Sumana, 30, explained simply, "I meditate." Sometimes sitting. Sometimes moving. He showed me his walking meditation. Very, very slowly, I try to replicate his movement – I roll from my heel to the toe and hold the opposite foot in the air before placing it down. I concentrate on the action. He explains that this type of practice, called *zingyan shouk chin*, will clear my mind. Help me to develop patience and acceptance. Useful, no doubt, on the course.

From each hole on the Mount Popa Golf Course, I could see the dramatic cylindrical Daung Kalat, a volcanic plug rising 737 meters from the flat, hot plain – by comparison, Malaysia's soaring Petronas Towers are 452 meters tall. (Nomenclature is a bit confusing, since photogenic Daung Kalat is generally referred to as Mount Popa, but in fact is a prominent and picturesque outcrop that sits on the southwest flank of Mount Popa, which at 1,518 meters is considerably higher.) Daung Kalat is said to be the expelled core of a volcano last active 2,500 years ago, and the ground around the course is strewn with pieces of petrified wood.

Paul Spencer Sochaczewski

An hour's drive from Mount Popa, Myint Naing has one of the easier jobs in the Myanmar forestry department. Since 1999 his task has been to protect the Zee-O Thit-Hla sacred forest, which has been a government forest reserve since 1988. No one has cut a tree during that period. Is it the fear of a three-year prison sentence that has kept this cool holy grove intact while its surroundings lie barren and baking? Or is its environmental integrity due to something mystical, something far beyond government control?

While the Zee-O Thit-Hla sacred forest might have government protection, I sense that its real power, and hence the reason it survives, lies in things that go bump in the night. Throughout Asia one hears stories. A jealous wife puts a black-magic curse on her husband's mistress that makes the woman go mad. A man coughs blood, and when doctors X-ray his lungs they find dozens of metal pins, put there by a sorcerer. A farmer spends the night in the forest and when dawn comes, villagers find that he has entranced a man-eating tiger into a cage.

Trouble is, it's awfully hard to actually meet some of these magic-imbued people – these surreal episodes always seem to take place "in a distant village, over the next hill."

When I ask what trouble could befall someone who violates the sanctity of this sacred forest in central Myanmar, I expect the usual generalizations – "you'll fall sick," or "bad things will happen." So I listen with a grain of salt when I hear that a farmer's house had burned down after he and a companion cursed and acted disrespectively in this holy grove midway between Mount Popa and Bagan. I figure it for just another Asian tale, an urban legend of the type told by cosmopolitan skeptics about curious (and superstitious) rural folks who live far from the sophisticated capitals. Such stories are common, but irritatingly hard to analyze – one would welcome a team of Mythbusters to put some scientific empiricism into reports about men who sell their children's souls, thereby enabling them to turn into *were*-pigs to get rich. To investigate stories about soldiers whose sacred amulets have enabled them to survive being shot. Men who magically "teleport" themselves from one point to another. People who eat glass. Even a car repair method that relies on incantations and prayers instead of mallets and soldering irons. My amateur attempts at busting these myths usually results in a stalemate due to too many degrees of separation – the person I'm talking with heard it from his sister-in-law who heard it from her hairdresser who heard it from someone in the pub – that kind of thing. So when I was told that the people who were punished for intruding on this sacred forest in this forgotten corner of Myanmar actually existed, I was skeptical.

"No, they're real," the village elder insists. "The unfortunate men were U Aung Khin and his son-in-law U Aye San. Want to meet them?"

I stroll amidst mature trees so large I can't put my arms around them, including several fine *ficus* trees, which are seldom found in the arid zone. Some 35 tree species have been catalogued in this oasis of green. Is Zee-O Thit-Hla a relict forest, the last example of a richer flora that existed prior to the speculated deforestation that accompanied the 11th- to 13th-century construction of the great temples of Bagan?

I am finally introduced to U Aye San, the man who allegedly broke the taboos concerning this sacred grove and suffered as a result. He is a middle-aged man who appears perfectly, well, normal. "My father-in-law, U Aung Khin, was acting eccentric the morning that we entered the sacred forest," U Aye San says. "Yes, we were disrespectful, but we didn't know we were breaking the taboo."

As any cop will tell you, ignorance is no excuse for breaking the law, and the stern spirit-policemen of Zee-O

Thit-Hla Forest served punishment. "A few hours after we returned to the village, I heard a commotion," Aye San explains. "U Aung Khin's house was burning. He was inside, and got burned. But it was very odd. The cooking fire had been extinguished. The fire apparently started spontaneously, among the dried toddy palm leaves."

I am introduced to the hapless father-in-law. Aung Khin is 84 ("my secret of long life is rice and toddy") and half deaf. Our translator shouts into his good ear but to no avail. He is either embarrassed to speak about the event, or his memory is gone. He cannot confirm or deny Aye San's story.

On departure, I ask Myint Naing, the Zee-O Thit-Hla forest guard, which is a stronger deterrent to villagers – the *nats* or the government. "The *nats*," he says without hesitation. "Definitely the *nats*."

In one sense, sacred forests fit my Cartesian, left-brained worldview – they act as watersheds, offer shelter for animals, are repositories for medicinal plants and, in an emergency and given the proper ceremonies, can provide timber to rebuild a village ravaged by fire.

But they are also places of magic. When I was a boy, I believed in gardens filled with unicorns and sprites and goblins. I know these special places existed – I saw them in my picture books and in my mind's eye.

The first time I played Mount Popa, in 1993, the course was in poor shape, with subtropical scrub growing rampant on the fairways and tee boxes made of concrete-hard dirt. The holes had rarely been moved from one point on the green to another, and as a result, due to regular rain and the footsteps of golfers, the area around the holes became a meter-diameter funnel, sort of like a drain to help balls reach the target.

In the late 1990s, the Mount Popa Golf Course was refurbished. The greens have been improved, but they are still tough because of their shape – mostly convex, like overturned saucers – so it's difficult to keep the ball on the green without it running off.

Wisely, the people who fixed up the course kept one quirky feature – the sand green on the par-4 5th hole.

This was the first time I had played on a sand green. My approach shot landed with a satisfying plop. The caddie lifted my ball, raked a path to the hole, and replaced my ball. I babied the putt and it went, oh, two feet. Finally, realizing what I had to do, I rammed a stroke of polo-like strength and the ball traveled all of five feet.

The most daring snake charmer in the world practices her skill in a Mount Popa cave. On the chosen morning the farmer's wife, not quite a snake priestess but more like a snake intermediary, leads a long, slow procession of villagers up the steep slopes of Mount Popa. Her neck and arms are dusted white with rice powder, she wears a loose-fitting muslin shirt over her faded sarong, she has said her prayers to the gods, and her soul has been blessed by the local Buddhist abbot. She has been given the assignment to beseech the Naga, the snake-god found throughout the subcontinent, to expedite the the monsoon rains.

Approaching the shallow cave where a king cobra is lurking, she moves slowly and respectfully, murmuring apologies for disturbing the snake-god's rest. She kneels in front of the reptile and touches her forehead to the ground three times, as the snake rears up and spreads its hood in alarm. The priestess serenely rises and undulates in slow, sensuous rhythms. using her body like a snake charmer's flute.

After several minutes of her trance-like dance, the priestess induces the cobra to strike. But the direction of the strike is predictable, and the woman steps back so that the cobra's fangs, ejaculating a teaspoonful of deadly venom, hit only her loose robe. The dance continues. The cobra strikes again and again, but the amount of venom that drips down the front of the woman's robe lessens with each strike. After five minutes the snake is thoroughly confused, weary, and frustrated, and exhausted of venom.

Approaching the cobra, whose head is still reared a meter off the ground, the woman gives the snake three quick kisses on top of its head. Bowing low, she murmurs her thanks to the Lord Naga and backs away slowly, as a commoner always takes leave of a king. The crowd, their tension relieved at last, follows the woman back down the mountain, small boys laughing and kicking up dust and villagers chatting. To the southwest, distant storm clouds gather over the Gulf of Martaban, soon to release their life-giving liquid to the parched rice fields below.

In this land where good fortune comes from surprising sources, the Mount Popa caddies invariably bring good luck. On one tree-lined hole, U Moe Ting stationed himself out of sight of the tee, halfway down the fairway, acting as fore-caddie to watch the flight of the ball in the (not unreasonable) expectation that I would hit an errant drive. I was certain that I sliced my ball into the forest, but when I arrived, U Moe Ting greeted me with "good news sir" and proudly pointed out my ball, which was not only sitting on the fairway but residing quite comfortably on a rare tuft of grass.

I felt that magic like that should be rewarded, and I left U Moe Ting my glove and half a dozen balls.

## CRYPTO-GOLF

I'm intrigued by Burma's seldom-visited golf courses, a British legacy that survives in unusual places. For me this is crypto-golf; golf where it oughtn't be. Some of the highlights of my ongoing quest to play all of these isolated courses follow:

It was a rainy weekday in December, with southern Burma receiving the tail end of Typhoon Durian that had swept through Southeast Asia, when I appeared at the Kawthaung Golf Club and asked for a game. The manager, U Naing Htay, reluctantly agreed to brave the elements and accompany me, later telling me that I was the first foreigner to grace his attractive course.

Whether or not this is true (and I have my doubts), the point is that good golf, at a refreshingly low price and in friendly company, can be found throughout Burma.

The Texas-sized country of 53 million people, which had a British colonial past, has 102 courses, according to Duncan Weir, director of golf development at the Royal and Ancient, a group based in Scotland that promotes golf worldwide.

Some of these courses are of international standard, such as the Gary Player-designed Pun Hlaing Golf Club in Yangon, the country's largest city, and up until recently, its capital.

But I became intrigued by the large number of isolated, quirky, smaller courses sprinkled throughout the country, for years ruled by a military junta not known for its sense of humor or pursuit of aimless pleasure. This, for me, is classic crypto-golf – golf where it oughtn't be.

On many of these "distant greens," grass was bare or shaggy, the fairways too rectangular, the bunkers overgrown. The greens were made of sand (locally called "browns"), and the golf clubs I was offered sometimes resembled garden implements more than the expensive clubs I have at home. But then I reminded myself that I was playing on empty courses, paying less than a dollar in green fees, and, if U Naing Htay at Kawthaung was right, breaking new ground.

In Katha, where George Orwell wrote *Burmese Days*, a golf course meanders through a teak forest, and if you're lucky you will get an extra bounce by hitting one of the two concrete helicopter landing pads on the first fairway.

Myitkyina, in northern Burma near the Chinese border, boasts two golf courses. Soe Myint, the manager of the 9-hole Myitkina Golf Club, took special pride in pointing out one of the course's more diabolical design features, which I found on several courses – elevated greens shaped like upturned saucers.

And in Mawlaik, on the Chindwin River and accessible only by river, Scottish teak planters built a nine-hole course in 1936 with two sand greens. Members proudly say it's the oldest (or second oldest or third oldest, no one is quite sure) course in the country. Local rules allow a free drop if your ball lands in the droppings of a wandering water buffalo.

During the pre-Democracy era, I had heard stories about one of the world's most exclusive golf courses, the Royal Myanmar Golf Club, at the vast and isolated new capital Naw Pyi Taw, midway between Yangon and Mandalay. The course was built for the ruling generals in 2010, and while I had little interest in breaking bread with those men, I was curious to play there. I got my chance in 2016.

Businessmen seeking government contracts regularly play at The Royal Myanmar Golf Club; it is said that the betting is for high stakes and the government officials playing with the businessmen rarely lose. The club hosts events for high-ranking visitors – the conference room sports a large banner proclaiming: "Gold Through Golf – The 9th ASEAN Navy Chiefs' Meeting" – but civilians are now welcome. There were a handful of foreign golfers on the course when I played on a warm Saturday morning in April.

It's an easy course, in good condition with well-maintained, slow greens. I particularly enjoyed the par-3 7th hole, a long uphill hole that vaguely resembles a volcano. From the green on the top, the view is lovely, and although I don't wish to overcook a metaphor, seems to reflect the state of Myanmar today. I was standing on the top, where the country's power brokers putt, while below off-duty caddies were hand-weeding the fairways. I saw a long pond, bordered by forest and rich in biodiversity. The shape of the hole itself reminded me of the replica of Yangon's famous Shwedagon stupa that has been built in Naw Pyi Taw. The construction of the clubhouse appears grandiose, but on closer inspection it is already falling apart – the glass was smeared with dirt and grime and the ATM was out of order, as was the WiFi. It is also poorly thought out – the floor of the shower area is paved with slippery white tiles, a health hazard in most countries. The restaurant serves the blandest fried noodles in Southeast Asia, perhaps a reflection that Myanmar's food is underwhelming – paradoxically Myanmar lies between three of the world's great food countries – India, China, and Thailand. My caddie spoke no English and was obviously new in the job. But no doubt she will learn quickly, as so many other young Myanmar women and men are doing, and no doubt the minor imperfections will be resolved, and no doubt the cooking skills will improve, and no doubt the natural landscape will be protected throughout the country.

# BORNEO TO BE WILD

A visionary zillionaire has built a diabolical, eco-feel-good, fuzzy-spiritualistic (and vegetarian) course.

---

## SARAWAK, Malaysia

"MANY OTHER GUESTS?" I ASK AS I CHECK IN AT THE open-air reception area of the Hornbill Golf and Jungle Club at Borneo Highlands.

"Just you," the smiling lady replies.

I had heard about the $100 million Borneo Highlands project created by Malaysian businessman Tan Sri Lee Kim Yeow and had always wanted to play at the golf course he built in the mountains of the Malaysian state of Sarawak, not far from the Indonesian province of Kalimantan. I just hadn't expected to be the only guest.

I was curious not just because the course was reputed to be lovely and tough, but because all of Tan Sri's projects come with a fuzzy eco-feel-good agenda.

But in order to commune with nature I have to first drive an hour south from the charming Sarawak capital of Kuching and, at the foot of the Penrissen mountain range, climb into a comfortable four-wheel-drive van for a half-hour journey to the 62-room hilltop resort, perched at 950 meters (3,100 feet).

As the driver burns the clutch up the steep incline, he

explains that before Tan Sri Lee dropped a bundle, all that existed here was a dirt track used by timber trucks to extract valuable tropical hardwoods from the mountainside.

I was curious whether Lee's vision would work in Sarawak. The Malaysian businessman, who is probably worth more than a medium-sized African country, earned lots of press when he turned an ugly, disused, open-cast tin mine outside of Kuala Lumpur, Malaysia, into the luxurious Mines Resort and Golf Club, which set a standard for creating golf courses out of ecologically damaged land. Tan Sri Lee (Tan Sri is a title bestowed by Malaysia's king that is similar to a knighthood) then turned his moneyed alchemy here to the Malaysian state of Sarawak, on the island of Borneo, a two-hour flight due east from the Malaysian capital. He bought a huge patch of rainforest that had been partially logged years earlier, and invested a bundle to turn the site into what he describes as "heaven on earth."

I actually had a second motive for visiting – this was a homecoming of sorts. I had first lived in Sarawak in 1969 as a Peace Corps volunteer. That was before timber operators had begun to seriously chop up Sarawak's rainforests, among the oldest on earth. Today, logging roads criss-cross much of the state, three times as large as Switzerland, and up to 70 percent of the forests, according to one observer, has been destroyed or damaged. Having spent much of my career working for a nature conservation organization and writing about environmental problems, I was curious whether golfing-oriented restoration ecology could provide a bit of environmental good news.

I dine alone at the resort's open-air vegetarian restaurant and order the yummy fried rice. I'm impressed that a virtually empty resort functions so well – staff who could easily have slacked are alert and friendly.

Many of the staff at Borneo Highlands come from the Anna Negri longhouse at the base of the mountain. I had visited the longhouse several years previously, following in the footsteps of a much more important visitor.

In 1855 British explorer, naturalist, and self-described "beetle collector" Alfred Russel Wallace trekked among Bidayuh longhouses scattered along the Sadong River, an area he described as "the Himalayas in miniature." Wallace was in Sarawak as the guest of James Brooke, the "white rajah of Borneo," and his collections of "natural productions," including seventeen orangutans, helped Wallace develop his theory known as the Sarawak Law, which set the stage for his later development of the theory of natural selection.

On this trek I went slowly, accompanied by my friend Bob, taking three days and staying in many of the same longhouse locations in which Wallace stayed.

Much of Sarawak's forest has been battered, but in this corner of the state, the scenery is similarly idyllic to that described by Wallace. "The descent ... was very fine," he wrote. "A stream, deep in a rocky gorge, rushed on each side of us, to one of which we gradually descended, passing over many lateral gulleys and along the faces of some precipices by means of native bamboo bridges."

Today these communities, where Wallace entertained children with finger shadows, have running water, electricity, and TV – American professional wrestling is particularly popular. They also have cars, prompting more than one longhouse resident to ask, "Why are you walking? Got road now, can drive there."

The trek ends at Anna Negri longhouse, set at the foot of the steep road that leads up to the deliciously difficult golf course at the Borneo Highlands Resort. When Wallace visited (the longhouse was then called Senna), he generated considerable interest.

"Many of the women and children had never seen a white

man before, and were very sceptical as to my being the same color all over as my face," Wallace wrote in *The Malay Archipelago*. "They begged me to show them my arms and body, and they were so kind and good-tempered that I felt bound to give them some satisfaction, so I turned up my trousers and let them see the color of my leg, which they examined with great interest."

But Wallace was a gentle soul and he quickly made friends. He recalled trying to use the string game "cat's cradle" as an ice breaker, which he thought would be new to his hosts, and being surprised when the local boys showed they were far more expert than he was.

Over a cold beer, Allan Ananth Pandian, the resort's spa and recreations manager, shows me the list of birds that have been seen on the course — some 200 species — and I'm reminded of what my friend Jeffrey McNeely, chief scientist at IUCN (International Union for Conservation of Nature), had told me: "Sarawak is to biodiversity as St. Tropez is to the bikini."

I retire to my simply decorated room — Tan Sri Lee has decreed that visiting golfers do not need televisions or private showers. I fall asleep listening to the chirping-screeching-whistling night chorus of the rainforest, just steps away.

After a dreamless sleep I head out into the cool morning mist in an electric golf cart. I must have done something right in a previous life to be the only golfer on a course like this on such a fine morning.

The first few holes wind uphill, flanked by the forest. I quickly learn that a ball hit off the fairway gets sucked up by the vegetation, never to be seen again.

At the tee of the 512-meter (560-yard), par-5 4th hole, I gaze toward an uphill fairway. Just behind where I assume the green to be rises the dramatic triangular massif of Penrissen

Hill, clad in dark green forest. To the right of the tee, a rough track leads to the border with Indonesia, a ten-minute walk. This is jungle golf at its finest, rivaling Kauai's famous Princeville for beauty and challenge.

Like many holes on this course, the 4th is filled with hazards, not all visible. I hit a decent drive, but learn too late that I should have been either twenty yards shorter or longer since a (hidden) stream that runs across the fairway has swallowed my Srixon. I take a penalty drop and aim for a boulder placed right in the middle of the fairway, expecting to miss it. Oh my god, I hit it straight, "don't hit the rock, don't hit..." But I get a good ricochet. Next shot is not too bad, and by luck I miss the mostly unseen lake that guards the left side. Straight is good here, since the fairway of the 4th hole, like those of most of the holes on the course, is nestled between rainforest on both sides. As I hack uphill I come upon yet another unseen small stream that protects the narrow opening to the green. This is getting tricky. The fairway funnels toward the green, which means that the forest edges closer and closer to snare wayward shots. Just as I am about to make my approach, I hear a slow *pau, pau, pau* cry. I've written about this bird in *Soul of the Tiger* – it's a Diard's trogon, an important omen bird for Sarawak's Iban tribe. But I forget if its call means "blessings on your endeavor" or "danger ahead, turn back." In retrospect it must have been the latter, since my ball sails into the adjacent jungle.

I'm losing balls left and right, but I remember a conversation I had with Tan Sri Lee, who said, "Lord Buddha teaches us how to live in harmony, not only in this world but with the universe." Tan Sri Lee, looking relaxed in an old jogging suit and playing with his pet gibbon, added, "Material wealth has no relationship to how smart you are."

Well, my material wealth is suffering since I'm poorer by quite a few balls. But I'm starting to relax and heed his advice that "nature can heal us." And his Buddhist-influenced philosophy starts to make a lot of sense, since after all, golf is arguably the ultimate Zen challenge.

Nevertheless, my Zen calm goes walkabout on the 425-meter (465-yard), par-4 6th hole. It looks innocent enough, but the stream that meanders alongside the fairway also criss-crosses the hole several times – and of course I have no idea where the stream is. All I can do is whack and hope, whack and hope.

Although I'm the only player, I'm not alone.

I pass women hand-weeding the course, and one man who looks like he's auditioning for *Star Wars*. I inquire later and learn that he was wielding one of Tan Sri Lee's inventions to reduce the use of herbicides – a small "fire gun" to zap weeds.

I continue to whack and hope on the 510-meter (558-yard), par-5 11th, where I aim my downhill tee shot toward a small landing area in a rapidly narrowing fairway. Then I had to hit a blind second shot through a narrow gap between a boulder field, while keeping out of an unseen large pond that protects the green in front and on the right. Beautiful? Certainly. Challenging? Obviously. Fair? Hey, this is golf.

And so it goes. Australian golf architect Neil Crafter, with considerable assistance from Tan Sri Lee, has designed a course that mixes teeth-gnashing frustration ("how could they expect me to know there's a pond there") with spectacular beauty and touches of meticulous care – like the blue, white, and purple orchids, grown in Borneo Highlands' nursery, which frame the tee of the 5th hole.

I'd like to say that my golf improves as the round progresses, but that's not quite right. What happens is that my attitude and my perception improve. Maybe all this back-to-nature stuff is working.

It's midday and the afternoon rain clouds are starting to gather. Rainfall here is a staggeringly soggy 550 centimeters (216 inches) per year, which is about ten times the annual rainfall of London. This ever-present moisture posed a particular dilemma for Tan Sri Lee, who tries not to use chemicals on the course. Ong Chin Aun, Hornbill Golf's greenkeeper, explained that he had no choice but to use some fungicide on the greens. But all the fertilizer is organic, he assured me, and to get rid of worms on the greens they employ hungry chickens.

Maybe Tan Sri Lee has it right with his Doctor Feel-Good philosophy: "People and nature *can* coexist."

I feel suitably Zen-ish indeed as I stand on the tee of the 285-meter (311-yard) par-4 15th hole. Recalling Tan Sri Lee's admonition that "higher altitude means that you're closer to God," I stare, admiring the view, feeling vaguely like Zeus on Olympus. This hole pushes the concept of the elevated tee to nirvana-like proportions – the drop-off from tee to fairway is some 76 meters (83 yards)[10], a bit higher than the drop at the world-famous 17th hole at Greg Norman's The Experience on the Hawaiian island of Lanai. The Lanai course is a relatively frequently played course, and the 17th hole at The Experience is among the most photographed in the world. But I'm playing an empty and spectacular jungle course in Borneo, and that's enough inspiration for me to nail a drive. I then hit to the green where I find a fist-sized rhinoceros beetle having a siesta – when the sun hits its shiny dark brown body, the creature emits a metallic greenish tinge, like a 1950s hot rod.

I hear the unmistakable whoosh-whoosh of rhinoceros hornbills in flight, sounding like a steam train picking up speed. The rhinoceros hornbill is the most important bird for many Borneo tribes, and its presence also signifies a healthy forest.

---

[10] About the height of a 25-story building.

After my round, I ran into Tan Sri Lee again and asked about the bird. He smiled broadly. He may have spent nine figures on a remote jungle outpost. His resort may be empty. But ...

"The hornbills are back," Tan Sri Lee explained, taking credit for the black and white *kenyalang*. "We used golf to repair nature."

# PUTTING THE BOUNCE
# INTO THE BALL

Playing golf near the rainforest
that revolutionized the game.

## MANAUS, Brazil

**N**ORMALLY WHEN I PLAY GOLF, I CLUTTER MY HEAD
with an excess of swing thoughts – turn, extend the
arm, hit toward two o'clock.

But standing on the first tee of the Manaus Golf Club
outside the Brazilian city of Manaus, I complicated my life
even more by posing a historical conundrum – if Manaus had
never existed, would we still be playing golf with featheries?

With all that mental baggage, my first drive on this hilly
course was not a thing of beauty.

Still, I was delighted to be in this Amazonian heart of
Brazil, a five-hour flight inland from the sensual coastal city
of Rio.

Manaus, population 1.8 million, owes its fame to two
lucky breaks of nature. The first is its location, at the confluence
of the vast Solimoes River and the similarly huge black-water
Rio Negro. These two riverine behemoths join at Manaus to
form the mighty Amazon, a river so big it carries one fifth of
all the fresh water in the world; in one day it carries more

fresh water than the Thames in England carries in a year. An adventurer who wanted to kayak the length of the Amazon from its source in Peru claimed he had to keep paddling a hundred kilometers out to sea before he could taste salt water. With its strategic location, positioned in the middle of the vast Amazon rainforest, Manaus was well placed to become an important inland port that enabled traders, explorers, and beetle collectors to open the interior of South America.

The second gift of nature to Manaus is that its surrounding forests are rich in natural rubber.

The course was deserted on the Tuesday afternoon I played, but the club secretary, Celso Sato, had organized for me to play with Denilson Macado, the caddymaster.

Although he's only been playing for four years, Denilson, 26, has a fluid swing and plays off four.

He was beating me handily. But I had a good excuse.

With my wife and a friend, I had just returned from two weeks exploring the upper Rio Negro in an open canoe, following the route of Alfred Russel Wallace, the mid-19th-century British naturalist. We had been sleeping in hammocks in Indian villages, swimming in the black waters, and seeking remnants of traditional culture that hadn't been expunged by Christian missionaries. Great fun, but I was exhausted.

I thought I had left the jungle behind, but as we stood on the tee box of the 5th hole, I was surprised to see a mini-forest, smack in the middle of the fairway. This wasn't just a few decorative bushes, this was a patch of some two dozen good-sized trees, about 130 yards (118 meters) from the tee.

I remembered the advice of my caddie I had in Thailand, related in Part II. "Left side no good," she scolded. And her advice would have been appropriate in Manaus, since the left side contained bunkers and scrub. "Right side no good," she had also admonished. True again, because on the right of the fairway forest was a small bunker, and just next to it was out of bounds. No chicken-out zone. "Straight good." Denilson smacked a drive that somehow weaved between the palms. I punched a drive that landed in the middle of them, but I had a line to the green.

I found it rather refreshing to have a forest in the middle of a fairway, here at the epicentre of the Amazon.

But I was disappointed that there were no rubber trees on the course, and my mind drifted again toward tales of how the British had ambushed and almost destroyed Manaus.

Manaus became rich because of a single tree, found only in the Amazon rainforest: *Heavea brasiliensis*. Rubber.

The discovery of rubber in this region corresponded with the industrial revolution, and the two concepts fed each other. At its peak, rubber financed a civic flowering in which the citizens of Manaus enjoyed electricity and public trams around the time that major European cities first adopted these innovations.

In an anecdote that local historians swear is true but that still sounds like an urban legend, the richest of the rich would send their laundry to Lisbon, since they feared the tea-colored local water would stain their delicate bedclothes.

During the rubber boom in the 1880s, Manaus built the elegant *Teatro Amazonas* opera house, with roofing tiles from Alsace, furniture from Paris, marble from Carrarra, steel from England, and 198 chandeliers, 32 of which were crafted from Murano glass.

World-class singers from Europe performed, the first of which featured Enrico Caruso in 1897. He returned safely to Europe, but other visiting troupes lost up to half their entourage to yellow fever. The streets surrounding the theater were paved with rubber so that theatergoers would not be disturbed by the clip-clop of horses' hooves.

And then the British screwed things up for the Brazilians.

In 1876, a British agent named Henry Wickham (described by some as a "bio-pirate") smuggled 70,000 rubber seeds from the forests near Manaus and sent them to London's Kew Gardens, where they were propagated and subsequently dispatched to British colonies in South and Southeast Asia. Unlike the Brazilians, who harvested the milky sap from the wild trees, the British figured out how to domesticate and grow rubber as a cash crop on vast plantations. Even today, in Malaysia and other countries, it is a common sight to see dark, orderly rows of *Hevea* trees aligned like soldiers in formation and stretching over vast vistas. Rubber agriculture in the British colonies flourished, while the Brazilian rubber business, based on arduously harvesting an unreliable wild crop far from any seaport, crashed.

"Rubber has certainly changed sports," I mentioned to Denilson.

"Sure," he nodded. "Without *borracha* we'd have no footballs."

"What about rubber in golf balls?"

"That's good too. Your honor."

I stood on the tee of the par-3 6th hole and hit a pretty nice 7-iron to the edge of the green, surrounded by bunkers.

"*Uma boa tacada*," Denilson said. Good shot. "But wrong green."

Challenged by limited space for his nine-hole layout, Brazilian architect Nelson Ferreira had to be creative to make it interesting for players going around a second time to complete the 18. On some holes he took the easy way out, by providing alternative tee boxes. But on a few holes Ferreira got creative and built two completely separate greens.

I checked the plaque next to the tee box. T. Miyaki had a hole-in-one on this hole, as did N. Mizamoto, not to mention M. Okamura, and Y. Kaito and ...

Denilson saw my curious expression. "Just about all our hundred members are Japanese."

Brazil boasts the largest ethnic Japanese population out-side of Japan, and many of the members of the Manaus Golf Club are third and fourth generation *nikkei* who manage fac-tories in the city's tax-free zone. Production of televisions and toasters has replaced rubber as the commercial savior of this metropolis in the rainforest.

On the seventh hole, Denilson's favorite, we stood on the tee and gazed toward a huge orange ball of a setting sun. Hidden frogs made froggish noises, a flock of red parrots screeched overhead, and when I turned back I saw that a full moon had risen.

It was a beautiful afternoon and I was playing like a jerk.

I was so tired that it was easy to become philosophical.

"Denilson, rubber has revolutionized golf," I said. "Rub-ber is what makes golf balls go far."

We headed toward the 8th tee. "Denilson, all golf balls use rubber, don't they?"

Denilson looked at the brand name of my ball. "*A minha bola é melhor do que a sua, porque é feita de borracha.*" My ball is made from rubber, but not yours, he said.

Surprised, I pulled out another ball of a different brand. "What about this one?"

"*Sim. Essa também é boa.*" That one is ok.

Now I had a great excuse for slicing my drives – up to now I had been using a ball that was made of synthetic rubber.

I learned a few weeks later that my question was stupid and Denilson's answers were wrong. Neither Denilson's ball, nor the new one I put in play, contained any natural rubber at all.

"No golf balls today use natural rubber," Tom Kennedy, of Top Flite Golf Company, confirmed. All the balls we play – and that includes balls used by the pros and the weekend hackers – are made of synthetic rubber and plastic.

I asked Kennedy, the company's senior vice-president of research and development, to walk me through the evolution of golf ball design.

Initially golf balls, called featheries, were made of leather stuffed with goose feathers. Adequate, but with hardly any bounce and with the aerodynamics of a wet sock.

Then, in 1843, a Brit named William Montgomerie sent samples of a natural latex called gutta-percha, derived from the dried gum of the Malaysian sapodilia tree, to scientists in London. They demonstrated that the rubber-like substance could be molded after heating in hot water, but on cooling regained its original strength and resilience (and Michael Faraday discovered that gutta-percha was an excellent electrical insulator, making possible the practical applications of electricity and the telegraph – developments that revolutionized the world).

About 1845, the first gutta-percha golf ball was made by Robert Paterson of St. Andrews in Scotland.

Soon thereafter, natural rubber provided the rubber thread windings for a new generation of balls, covered with gutta-percha. With this revolutionary ball, made of an outer from Malaysian natural rubber and an inner core from Brazilian natural rubber, hackers started to see their drives sail previously unimaginable distances.

The next evolution came around 1903 when the gutta-percha cover was replaced by balata, originally obtained from the milky latex of the *Manilkara bidentata* tree, found from Mexico to Brazil. Then, during the 1930s, a process was developed to vulcanise the balata, which strengthened the material.

The natural rubber era ended when synthetic balata, developed in the 1960s, replaced natural balata, and today all contemporary golf balls use various forms of synthetic rubber.

But as I said, I didn't know all that at the time. So, on the 8th tee and quite willing to believe that Denilson knew what he was talking about, I switched to a ball he claimed had a core of natural rubber.

And I got hot.

On the 8th hole, a 340-meter (371-yard) dogleg right, I hit a solid drive. I was a bit nervous about the second shot because this green, like most on this course, is shaped like an inverted saucer and poor approaches won't hold. I landed just short, pitched to about two yards, missed my par putt by a few inches, and had a tap-in bogey.

"Pretty good, this rubber ball," I said, laughing.

The par-3 9th hole is another of those holes with two greens – the 9th plays to an elevated green protected by deep bunkers 160 meters (175 yards) away, the companion 18th green is shorter, at 140 meters (153 yards), both requiring tee shots over water.

This time I drove toward the correct green but landed in the bunker in front of the green. Got out cleanly. Pushed my par putt a foot past the hole for another tap-in bogey, just as the sun set.

I now know that my ball didn't contain one molecule of natural rubber. But I'm not proud – I'll take whatever assistance I can, and tap-in bogeys are fine. And now I even have a new swing thought – rubber core, rubber core, rubber core.

# NAPALM BE GONE

That boom you hear in Vietnam is
an explosion of golf courses.

## DALAT, Vietnam

**M**Y FAVORITE GOLF COURSE IN VIETNAM OWES ITS
existence to a puppet king, a French architect who
restored Roman ruins, and a rich American who
craved virgins.

I spent part of the Vietnam War period protesting it, along
with my fellow high-minded and moderately spoiled
American university friends. Then, after we got rid of
Lyndon Johnson only to watch Bobby Kennedy get shot and
Richard Nixon elected, I entered the United States Peace
Corps, which at that time offered a deferment to the conflict
we considered unjust and "not our problem."

I was assigned to Sarawak, a Malaysian state on the island
of Borneo. Just a short hop across the South China Sea from
Vietnam, as it turned out.

During those heady, full-of-life days I never thought that
I would eventually love the sport of golf or go to Vietnam to
play it.

But golf in Vietnam is booming, and it has become a travel-writer's cliché to point out the irony that the Ho Chi Minh Trail, which Americans tried so hard to napalm into oblivion (the Vietnamese refer to the conflict as the "American War"), has now been renamed the Ho Chi Minh Golf Trail and features courses that would not be out of place in such high-ticket golf destinations as Hawaii, Spain or nearby Thailand.

According to Nguyen Ngoc Chu, general secretary of the fledgling Vietnam Golf Association, Vietnam currently has 17 golf courses, with plans to bring the total up to one hundred, about half the number of Asian golf behemoths like Thailand and Indonesia.

Recognizing this growth and the quality of the courses, at their December 2007 meeting in Cancun, Mexico, the International Association of Golf Tour Operators designated Vietnam as the "undiscovered golf destination of the year."

The Dalat Palace Golf Club seems to be everyone's favorite course in Vietnam. Partly it's the intelligent and challenging layout, partly the mature vegetation, partly the numerous hills and lakes. But what is truly delightful is that Dalat, altitude 1,500 meters (4,900 feet), is a city of eternal spring, making it a welcome retreat to the pollution and hustle of Ho Chi Minh City and Hanoi.

The golf course at Dalat played a key role in Vietnam's golf history.

Bao Dai[11], the last of the Nuyen kings, encouraged construction of the course.

French-educated Bao Dai commissioned Ernest Hébrard, who redesigned the Greek city of Thessaloniki, Greece, after the Great Fire of 1917, and upgraded Casablanca and restored Diocletian's palace at Split in Croatia to design Dalat town.[12] In 1922 Hébrard allotted space on Doi Cu Hill for a golf course.

Due to the rigors of World War II and the burgeoning Vietnamese independence movement, by the time of Bao Dai's abdication in 1945, the course at Dalat was abandoned. Jim Sullivan of Mandarin Media, who helped coin the phrase Ho Chi Minh Golf Trail, notes that when local golfer Dao Huy Hach wanted to revive the course in the late 1950s, "he had to rely on aerial photos to pick out the putting surfaces" amidst the overgrown vegetation.

What's the reason for Vietnam's golf boom?

Vu Van Yen, deputy editor of *Vietnam Golf* magazine, felt that a strong economy, aided by Vietnam's entrance to the World Trade Organization, is a major locomotive of the golf boom. She estimates that the number of golfers in Vietnam is growing at fifteen percent a year.

The tourism numbers are also robust. The World Travel and Tourism Council (WTTC) predicted that Vietnam would be among the top ten tourist destinations in the world by 2016.[13]

---

[11] Widely seen as being a puppet ruler serving French, and later Japanese, interests.

[12] Likely at the urging of the French, who wanted a cool retreat from the miasma of Saigon.

[13] Which was a touch optimistic; in 2013 Vietnam was ranked 29th in the world, and 10th in Asia.

But will Vietnam face a golf course bubble?

Absolutely not, says Nguyen Ngoc Chu, whose Vietnam Golf Association is linked to the country's Ministry of Culture, Sports, and Tourism. "Germany, with a similar area and population to Vietnam, has 656 golf courses," Chu notes. "We now have 8,000 Vietnamese golfers and that number is growing – and it's still early days."

A friend and I were drinking in Larry's Bar at the elegant Dalat Palace Hotel and I asked who the "Larry" was who gave the pub its name.

Turns out that a man named Larry Hillblom spent $40 million to restore the Dalat Palace Hotel and the Dalat Palace Golf Course – he could be considered the financial godfather of the current Vietnamese golf boom.

In the annals of rogues, scoundrels, and guys whose life story would make a terrific Coen brothers movie, Larry Hillblom's true story is better than fiction.

Hillblom was a millionaire many times over – he founded and was the "H" in the courier and air freight company DHL. Besides golf he had another passion – he enjoyed deflowering young women, paying big money to madams in Vietnam, the Philippines, and Micronesia for certified virgins.

When Hillblom died, numerous women who said they bore children by Hillblom made a claim for his estate.

These women and children faced two obstacles – Hillblom did not acknowledge the illegitimate children in his will, and he disappeared in a plane crash leaving behind no DNA. Rather surreally, his home and office in Saipan, Micronesia, had been wiped clean of anything – a piece of hair, sweat on a sheet, a dirty Q-tip – that could have been used to prove paternity. What's more, the sinks had been scrubbed with muriatic acid, and toothbrushes, combs, hairbrushes, and clothes were found buried in the backyard, making them useless for DNA testing.

Considerable money was at stake. Eventually a judge ordered Hillblom's brother and mother to submit to genetic testing. After a lengthy court battle, four children from the Philippines, Vietnam, and Micronesia were awarded $90 million apiece.

Golf was put on hold during the various Vietnam wars. Nevertheless, American golfer Billy Casper, in Vietnam on a USO tour to bolster troop morale, played a round in Dalat with golfer Dao Huy Hach in 1966, several months before Casper beat Arnold Palmer to win that year's U.S. Open. "The course looked like it was just carved out of the dirt," Casper said.

Golf hasn't had smooth sailing in this Communist country, which only in the last decade or so has embraced a capitalistic surge.

Nguyen Ngoc Chu notes that golf had to receive an official Communist Party endorsement that playing a game so closely associated with capitalism and colonialism was acceptable. Because teachers in Vietnam only earn about $150 a month, and the prime minister's salary is just $300 a month, Chu notes, golf was seen as a rich man's pastime and had to be repositioned as being socially acceptable.

The breakthrough came in the early 1990s, according to Chu, when former Foreign Minister Nguyen Manh Cam attended a regional meeting and felt isolated when the other diplomats went off to play golf. Abdullah Ahmad Badawi, then Malaysia's foreign minister (and later Malaysia's prime minister), took Cam aside and encouraged him to learn to speak English and to play golf.

Nguyen Manh Cam returned to Hanoi and promoted golf among his colleagues. He had to overcome resistance, Chu notes, including a fear that golf courses will "take land from the people." (In fact, one of the dark sides to the current Vietnam golf boom is that land grabs have occured in which the local government gives the green light for private golf developers to buy land from villagers, often at prices favorable to the developers.) Foreign Minister Cam helped to set up an informal golf academy for high-level government officials. He took Abdullah Ahmad Badawi's advice to heart; he now speaks English, is honorary president of the Vietnam Golf Association, and plays golf off an 18 handicap.

Attractive golf courses can be found throughout the country, a long, skinny nation (shaped like a dragon, the Vietnamese like to say), which covers a latitude shift greater than that of Bangkok to Singapore. Many new layouts, several involving superstar architects like Jack Nicklaus and Greg Norman, are on the way. With such a variety, I asked Chu which course is the best. Chu, a mathematician with a philosopher's bent and a diplomat's smile replied, "A golf course is like a lady. Each one is beautiful in her own way."

It's a clichéd truism that military bunkers in Vietnam have been replaced by the less-martial golfing variety. Nevertheless, this concept is particularly valid in the region of China Beach, near Danang, in the center of the country. The long strip of white sand was initially a major Vietcong redoubt and later a much-appreciated R&R site for American GIs – during the war, U.S. soldiers near Danang created a small golf course using C-ration cans as cups and red sand for greens.

Vietnam vets will recall that China Beach isn't far from

the hamlets of My Lai and My Khe where, on March 16, 1968, the American 11th Brigade, following General William Westmoreland's strategy of "flushing out" the Vietcong, massacred 504 Vietnamese civilians during a four-hour killing spree.

The Vietnamese are nothing if not pragmatic. Today, My Lai and My Khe are located near two of the country's most prestigious courses – the Colin Montgomerie-designed Montgomerie Links and the Greg Norman-designed Danang Golf Club.

Just as the Vietnamese have embraced "Market-Leninism," they seem rather unemotional about the construction of a major resort near a killing field that was once in the heartland of Vietcong territory. Pham Thanh Cong, 50, My Lai museum director, was one of only five survivors of the My Lai massacre – he survived by hiding under the corpses of his mother, sisters, and seven-year-old brother, according to James Pringle of the *International Herald Tribune*.

"Yes, we are happy at the prospect of more foreigners coming," Pham is reported as saying. "We want them to see the tragedy that occurred, but also to enjoy themselves in Vietnam. New development creates employment, and helps improve peoples' lives."

# STEPPES-TO-HEAVEN

"Natural golf" roams the range in Mongolia.

—————⋈⋈—∘

## ULAANBAATAR, Mongolia

O NCE MY TAXI LEFT THE CHARMLESS CAPITAL OF Mongolia, with its stolid Soviet-era apartment blocks and busy personality-challenged streets, the road seemed to abruptly head toward the steppes. Put another way, the road headed nowhere – I got the distinct impression, true as it turned out, that if we kept driving we would become as lost and dispirited as the Flying Dutchman of Wagner's opera.

I wanted to play golf at the Ulaanbaatar Resort Golf Club – a rather grand name for a remarkably modest course, considering the tees were beat-up Astroturf, the fairways were ragged, and the greens were sand mixed with oil.

The handful of golf courses in Mongolia are so natural that at first glance they seem to be an extension of the endless steppes that characterize this big sky country. These broad, mostly barren, somewhat flat vistas, generally set against a deep-blue sky – sometimes dotted with camels, horses, and goats, and rarely perturbed by roads or towns – give me a bizarre feeling. It is agoraphobia, the antithesis of claustrophobia. There is so much emptiness that my urbanized eye doesn't know where to focus. I long for landmarks. There is too much nothing.

Of course one man's nothing is another creature's home-on-the-range. Mongolia's grassland steppes, so similar to the golf course I was playing on, are home to some of the world's rarest and most endangered wildlife. The Mongolian wild ass, the golden eagle, the two-humped Bactrian camel. The Mongolian gazelle, gray wolf, and wild reindeer. Siberian marmot and saiga antelope. Six species of cranes (half the world's species of these iconic birds), and, in the distant hills, amidst the rocks and caverns and waterfalls of the omnipresent wilderness, lives the snow leopard.

I was in Mongolia at the request of WWF-World Wide Fund for Nature to help them develop a communications plan, and to train their staff to tell a story without being boring. I flew west across the country to the provincial town of Khovd, flying for three hours over terrain that was bereft of roads. It would have been a tedious four- to five-day drive.

A few hours' jeep ride outside of Khovd, I encountered a deep-throat, steppe-based, conservation-oriented spy story.

The taxi dropped me off at a small building half an hour outside Ulaanbaatar. Inside the modest clubhouse, I said hello to a group of three Japanese golfers who had just completed their round.

"How was it?" I asked.

They gave me hearty, conspiratorial laughs. "Wait til you see the bunkers," one of the men said. "And the greens," added another.

In the autumn of 2004, Gantulga Sharav, a park ranger who is head of a Mongolian anti-poaching unit, got a call on his mobile phone from a man I will call Mr. Z, who said, "There's a story going around that a guy in my village killed a snow leopard."

"Mr. Z." is one of some 160 conservation spies in three western Mongolian provinces. Usually referred to in Mongolian by more politically neutral descriptors like "volunteer ranger," "public conservationist," and "reporter," these men provide information on poaching to conservation rangers. Even though it is unlikely that Mr. Z.'s enemies will read this book, I agreed not to use his name to protect his cover.

Based on Mr. Z.'s report, Gantulga Sharav and a policeman drove to the temporary camp in the mountains where the alleged poacher, Iriimed, was living for the summer season. Their conversation went something like this.

"We heard you killed a snow leopard," Sharav said.

"Nope," Iriimed replied.

"Well, you won't mind if we look around."

And in the shed next to Iriimed's *ger* they found a fresh snow leopard skin.

"Why did you do it?"

"The animal killed twenty of my sheep," Iriimed complained.

Iriimed was unable to show any sheep carcasses or bones and finally admitted poaching the rare snow leopard, whose skin might have brought him $200 if sold underground in Khovd.

The snow leopard has semi-mythological importance in Mongolia and is legally protected, and it is one of the world's most elusive and endangered mammals. There are only 3,500–7,000 of the animals left in a 12-country swathe of mountainous Central Asia and the Himalaya, according to the International Snow Leopard Trust, with Mongolia home to some 800–1,200 of the big cats.

A 2003 report released by TRAFFIC, WWF, and the International Snow Leopard Trust found a sharp rise in hunting in the 1990s to supply the black market. The leading threats to the animals, which are more endangered than tigers, are trade in bones (used in Chinese traditional medicine), sale of furs, and retaliatory killing by herders protecting their livestock.

As our two-car caravan criss-crossed the flat steppes of the Khar Us Nuur National Park, two things struck me. I was intrigued that this desolate landscape was relatively rich in rare wildlife – Altai mountain sheep, saiga antelope, Siberian ibex, snow leopard, and other threatened species. And I was reassured that in our crowded planet such a seemingly empty vastness could exist.

Mongolia, which is roughly three times the size of France, has a population of less than three million people, giving it the lowest population density of any country in the world. It seemed a place without primary colors – where nature's palette was limited to shades of gray, brown, and ochre, with some faded purple late in the day. It reminded me of the harsh moonscapes of Ladakh – a place of sand and rock and gravel inhabited by hardy horse-riding, and by throat-singing nomads whose herds of sheep, goats, and double-humped Bactrian camels send wisps of dust into the air.

Enkh Amgalan is general secretary of the Mongolian Golf Association. "Golf is in its early stages here," he noted without a touch of irony. "We have maybe a hundred Mongolian players, and about the same number of foreign golfers, mostly Koreans."

The leading proponent of Mongolian "natural golf," or play-ing on golf courses that fit naturally into the landscape, is Andre Tolme, a civil engineer from New Hampshire who golfed across Mongolia.

Following a route that might have been traversed by Chinggis Khan almost a thousand years earlier, Tolme hit 12,170 shots with his 3-iron, covering a distance of 1,985 kilometers in 90 days.

A few thoughts come to mind.

First, according to calculations based on Tolme's ac-count, his average shot was a remarkable 163 meters (178 yards) using a 3-iron (now retired to his closet). A 3-iron is a hard club to hit even on a manicured fairway, let alone on the rough surface of the Mongolian steppes, using battered balls and enduring wind, fatigue, dust, heat, and cold (and, I'm speculating of course, he was also fighting off the odd hangover from an excess of fermented mare's milk and the occasional gurgly tummy from a diet overly rich in mutton and meager on vegetables). Tolme plays off 15, a respectable handicap for a recreational golfer.[14]

Second, Tolme lost 509 balls, even though he said, "I mark the line like a Labrador retriever and then count my steps."

Third, by researching this story, I learned that the gerbil originated in Mongolia.

---

[14] Tolme did well; by comparison Australian golfer Adam Scott, who won the 2013 Masters and was World Number 1 for several months in 2014, hits his 3-iron 200 meters (220 yards) on well-maintained professional courses.

Andre Tolme suggests that Mongolia is the birthplace of golf. "Archeologists recently uncovered human remains in Central Asia that were covered in Tartan plaid fabric," Tolme notes. "Do we really need more evidence than this?"

My WWF friends and I camped by a stream of pure water, amidst a grove of willow trees just beginning to grow their spring leaves. We hiked up the river canyon to two waterfalls, a pathless climb over packed snow covering the stream, crossing rock fields, dancing on slippery boulders, and gingerly sidestepping on vertiginous sandy patches where a slip would lead to a nasty tumble down to the river. My Mongolian colleagues, some of whom were wearing flip-flops, seemed to jitterbug across the natural obstacle course; wearing my hiking boots, I opted for a more deliberate pace. It was the kind of scenery I love – wild, having seen few visitors, with rushing water to cleanse the accumulated frustrations and stresses of living in Bangkok, my home at the time.

We passed carcasses of domestic sheep and goats, dead animals that were evidence of one of the main conservation problems that Mongolia faces – the competition for habitat between domestic livestock and other wild grazing animals.

Tseveenravdan Damdindorj, director of the WWF office in Khovd, explained the dilemma.

The hotter and drier climate resulting from global climate change results in less grass on the steppes, forcing the nomads to graze their sheep and goats in protected areas designed for wildlife. In addition, there is an overpopulation of livestock, up to twice the carrying capacity in some areas, which forces out the wild ibex and saiga antelope. In effect, by moving their herds into the mountains, the nomadic herders provide a food-delivery service for the isolated snow leopards. Some angry herders from the steppes then hunt the big cats, which have eaten their domestic animals.

Nevertheless, Mongolia has taken some positive conservation steps. For example, some eleven percent of the country is designated as protected area, for example, with plans to protect thirty percent by 2030.

During his golf trek, Andre Tolme faced some bothersome natural hazards – marmots carrying bubonic plague, four types of poisonous snakes (one of which coiled around his ball, protecting it as if it were an egg), and swarms of flies and mosquitoes, of which he said, "I just ignore them no matter how many are covering my face, head, backpack, or golf club."

And he was intrigued by the "ironic artistry" in the juxtapositions of the two-word phrase "Golf Mongolia."

"When you think of Mongolia," he said, "the words dry, remote, undeveloped, and unpretentious come to mind. When you think of golf – verdant, lush, fanciful, pretentious."

"But most important," Tolme said, "I followed through on the expedition because of the consistent encouragement I received when suggesting the idea to friends, family, and strangers. Now I've learned that the encouragement was probably due to a subconscious strain of sadism that lies repressed in most people and surfaces occasionally to cajole others into performing random ridiculous acts in the name of human evolution."

Golf is hardly booming in the country, but there are some developments.

The Ulaanbaatar Resort Golf Club where I played has

closed. Two new courses, Chinggis Khan Golf Course and Zaan Terelj Golf Club, have been built in the Gorkhi-Terelj National Park, some 60 kilometers (36 miles) from the capital.

Tuul River Golf Club, some 20 kilometers (12 miles) from Ulaanbaatar, will open nine holes in the summer of 2011, with another nine holes planned.

And the most ambitious golf project is Mount Bogd Golf Club, a $30 million development of Sky Resort of Mongolia and funded by Hong Kong investors. The complex, on the outskirts of Ulaanbaatar, includes a ski resort being built with French and Italian assistance. It, too, is located in a pro-tected area (a questionable practice in most parts of the world) – in this case, the Bogd Khan Uul Strictly Protected Area, a UNESCO-designated biosphere reserve. According to Amardush Dorj of Sky Resort, the Sky Resort project uses a Czech-designed state-of-the-art water-recycling system to treat sewage; the treated water is used for irrigating the course in the summer and snow-making in the winter.

Part of the optimism about conservation in Mongolia is curi-ously related to the national admiration for Chinggis Khan, who lived from 1162 to 1227. Khan conquered the world's largest land empire, stretching from Hungary and Poland in the west, to Vietnam in the south, and to Korea in the east. In Mongolia today, his name and image are omnipresent; he can be found on the currency, a luxury hotel, and a high-society pub. A popular beer is named after him, as is a vodka. Even the best golf course in Mongolia is named after him. His face, sculpted with stones on a barren hillside, gazes down on the capital Ulaanbaatar and is clearly visible from the downtown Eldorado Golf Driving Range.

Mongolians choose to downplay Chinggis Khan's West-ern reputation as a mass murderer and instead position him as a visionary leader who promoted the rule of law, education (he is credited with developing a script for the Mongolian language), and freedom of religion. He is also credited with developing the first international postal system. Above all, he was a Super-Steppeman, a fearless conqueror who made Mongolians proud of their rugged, independent culture, in which nature permeates the country's music, legends, sports, and self-image. The memory of Chinggis Khan (as well as the country's Mahayana Buddhist faith and still-prevalent shamanism) reflects a collective pride in the empty and pristine steppes, frigid lakes, and the idyllic, clear rivers. (In 2011, the eco-reputation of Chinggis Khan got a back-handed boost when the Carnegie Institution's Department of Global Energy issued a study that concluded that by wiping out 40 million people, Khan may have scrubbed 700 million tons of carbon from the atmosphere – roughly the quantity of carbon dioxide generated in a year through global gasoline consumption. The decimation of entire civilizations by Mongol invaders during the 12th and 13th centuries meant that vast areas of farmland and pasture grew thick with trees through natural reforestation, which absorbed carbon dioxide from the atmosphere. It appears that genocide reduces climate change. An interesting proposition.)

"The Mongolian society's unconscious belief system evokes a form of oneness with nature," explains Gantulga Sharav, the park ranger who chases snow leopard poachers. "That's the reason why Mr. Z. works with us," Sharav says, referring to the conservation informant. "Yes, Mr. Z. earned money when the poacher was caught (some $150, which is fifteen percent of the fine imposed by the courts), but money wasn't the prime motive. He primarily did it because he loves nature."

At the Ulaanbaatar Resort Golf Club I rent Callaway clones. My caddie Uyanga, a sociable 18-year-old student who is learning Japanese at university, raked the sand green, the only level space around. No need for her to tell me whether it breaks left or right. The hole is permanently cemented into the center of the green. I miss the colorful instructions of Southeast Asian caddies: "Right one grip." "Left lip, careful, slippery." "Straight ok. But uphill, lah, don't be chicken."

Chinggis Khan and his marauding colleagues may also be responsible for one of the world's greatest genetic shifts. An international group of geneticists studying Y-chromosome data has found that nearly eight percent of the men living in the region of the former Mongol empire carry Y-chromosomes that are nearly identical – that is, they are Mongol genes. The study, published in the *American Journal of Human Genetics*, estimates that 0.5 percent of the male population in the world, or roughly 16 million people, carry Mongol genes.

In our world of platitudes and corporate jargon, where thousands of days of executive time are wasted in retreats to determine a collective (and generally wishy-washy) "mission statement," Chinggis Khan was brutally frank.

Steven Dutch, professor of natural and applied sciences at the University of Wisconsin–Green Bay, writes:

Some of the Mongol tribes were literate, so we have written collections of the history and traditions of the Mongols, as well as accounts by Persian and Chinese chroniclers. One of the most telling is Genghis Khan's purported value statement. During a respite from his campaigns, he once asked some friends what the greatest pleasure was. After they variously answered hunting, falconry, or archery, Genghis is reputed to have said: 'The greatest joy a man can know is to conquer his enemies and drive them before him. To ride their horses and take away their possessions. To see the faces of those who were dear to them bedewed with tears, and to clasp their wives and daughters in his arms.'

I have no idea how this links to golf.

Andre Tolme played a form of Zen golf. He tried to ignore the blisters, the incessant sun, the radiating pain in his shoulders, the upset stomach from drinking fermented mare's milk, and cheap vodka offered by the nomads.

"I am amazed at how easy it is to live very happily with very little, without gadgets and toys," he wrote. "When I meet people living in a yurt – a simple home in the countryside – they laugh, they joke, they all know how to have fun."

# V

---

# GOLF'S PARADOX

Can golf be green and clean?
What might the future hold?

# CAN GOLF BE GOOD
# FOR NATURE?

Solving the conundrum.

———✦———

## BANGKOK, Thailand

I PLAY GOLF. AND I AM COMMITTED TO NATURE CON-servation.

Is this an insolvable conundrum, or can the two passions be reconciled?

"Golf development is becoming one of the most unsustainable and damaging activities to people and the environment," notes Chee Yoke Ling, environment coordinator of the Third World Network. Beijing-based Chee, writing in *Third World Resurgence* magazine, argues that golf fuels "environmental damage, resource conflicts, and even the violation of human rights." The Malaysian-born environmentalist writes that some golf courses divert agricultural water to maintain turf, golf course chemicals contaminate underground water systems and pose health threats, and some courses damage ecologically sensitive locations.

Taking a more positive view, Greg Norman, the famous Australian golfer who now has his own golf course design business, acknowledges that "environmentalists frequently portrayed golf courses as 'chemical wastelands.'" However,

Norman adds: "Golf courses can be community assets. Not only can they elevate property values, create jobs, and provide tax revenues, they can also provide green spaces, filter air, purify water, and create wildlife habitat."

The undeniable fact is that golf is booming in Asia – there are an estimated 18 million golfers in Asia playing on 3,700 18-hole courses (more than a quarter of them built since 1990) according to the R&A, a St. Andrews, Scotland, organization that serves as the game's rules and development body. With many more courses under development throughout Asia, the question of whether golf can be good for the environment takes on greater importance.

Jeffrey A. McNeely, chief scientist of the Swiss-based IUCN-International Union for the Conservation of Nature and a keen golfer, recognizes the need for responsible golf development. "All land use has an impact on the environment – the trick is to minimize damage and, where possible, enhance natural values," he says. "While there is no standard global certification process, an increasing number of people in the conservation movement recognize that golf is here to stay and urge that golf courses take steps to improve the sites on which they are built. They can do it, but it takes some effort, planning, and commitment."

John MacKinnon, a prominent scientist and field biologist currently working for an EU-funded biodiversity conservation project in China, acknowledges that "golf is sometimes accused of being environmentally unfriendly." However, in his co-authored book, *Guidelines for Maximizing Biodiversity on Golf Courses*, published by the ASEAN Regional Centre for Biodiversity Conservation, MacKinnon argues that "golf and environment can easily develop side by side, and golf courses can serve as miniature nature reserves. Golf courses provide green breathing spaces in a concrete landscape, and the well-managed turf has many valuable service values – soil protection, water filtering, pollution fixation, and biodiversity conservation. A well-managed golf course can provide more environmental benefits than a poorly managed nature reserve."

There's an obvious reason why golf is often considered "bad." In Asia, golf is generally elitist, and elitism is a red flag for some people, smelling of arrogance and abuse of power.

Perception is a powerful mental state, often stronger than facts. I have intelligent friends who raise their eyebrows when I tell them that a golf course can be ecologically sensitive. But a change of feeling won't happen overnight; for many folks an "elitist" tag equates with evil, or at least with something that is politically incorrect – something that is a bit callous and insensitive and frivolous at a time when the world faces serious concerns. South Koreans, who are golf crazy and might be expected to understand a guy's need to relax on the course for a few hours, hounded a prime minister out of office in March 2006 for playing golf when many voters felt he should have been working.

And in 2008, U.S. President George W. Bush and South Korea President Lee Myung-bak decided to forgo their scheduled golf game because it was at the beginning of the current global economic recession and playing golf "would send the wrong signals," a U.S. presidential spokesman said to their respective countrymen, worried about their jobs. In these difficult times it can be bad public relations to be seen out playing golf when the leader should be working.

Certainly golf courses pay heavily for the elitist perception. But perception does not necessarily reflect truth.

So what *is* the truth?

Over the past few years, I set out to learn whether golf can, in fact, be a positive force for nature and people.

One of the problems, I soon learned, was that there are few criteria for determining "good" and "bad" golf courses.

While the United States and Europe have active environmental groups that provide advice and recognition for courses wanting to be environmentally responsible, courses in Asia have few options.

Audubon International, which is not related to the better-known National Audubon Society of the United States, has a certification scheme that "helps golf courses protect our environment and preserve the natural heritage of the game of golf." While they have amassed a long list of certified courses in North America, only five Asian courses – in China, the Philippines, and Singapore – have been certified.

In my travels I see some abuses. But I have also visited courses that show good eco-social management and a willingness to "do the right thing."

Certainly some Asian golf course owners will continue to encroach on protected areas, use too many chemicals, and disregard environmental regulations. And water use will continue to be a problem – a poorly designed golf course can use as much water as a small town. But increasingly, Asian courses are following the stricter standards of golf developers in the United States, Europe, and Australia. Why this new righteousness? Partly because it's the law (of course the relevant laws need to be sensible and enforced, as in Singapore), and partly because it makes good marketing sense for resort owners to position their courses as "green." And pragmatically, an environmentally friendly golf course can save money by reducing costs for energy, water, chemicals, and maintenance.

This concept is particularly apparent in the United States.

"The new reality for American golf is that water is far too precious to be squandered on a golf course," Ron Whitten wrote in *Golf Digest*. "As communities around the country cope with extended droughts, the notion of courses sporting lush, wall-to-wall green grass is no longer feasible, very likely socially unacceptable, and in some ways downright criminal. Indeed, even the idea of fully irrigated fairways may soon become a thing of the past. There's a distinct possibility that golf in the future will routinely be played on minimally irrigated fairways. Brown is the New Green is more than a marketing slogan. It's becoming a mindset."

So, is golf a sport that I can play with a clear conscience?

The answer is a resounding "perhaps." Depends on the course. Depends on the owner. Depends on lots of things. But the trend seems cautiously encouraging.

# THE QUEST FOR
# GREEN GREENS

Yes, they're out there, and they're pretty terrific.

---

## MANILA, Philippines

I STAND ON THE FIRST TEE AT MANILA SOUTHWOODS Golf and Country Club and admire the green fairways, the birds, the clean air, all so welcome compared to the pollution and havoc of downtown Manila.

Does this course signal the future of golf?

For years I have been on a journey in search of environmentally responsible golf courses. My quest has taken me to dozens of Asia's leading (and some rather obscure) golf courses to learn whether golf is the work of the Anti-Green Devil or blessed by Eco-Happy Angels.

I got mixed answers. Some Asian golf courses use too much water, spray too many chemicals, and steal land from neighboring villages. But I also found a growing number of golf course operators who care about the environment and who have shown that a well-managed golf course run by conscientious people can be good for nature.

When I asked friends familiar with Asian courses where I could find an eco-inspirational course, they pointed in the unlikely direction of Manila, the Philippines, hardly a city one thinks of as clean and green.

On the par-3 16th hole at the Legends Course of Manila Southwoods, I was pleased to see herons nesting in the vegetation growing alongside the lake. Unlike many courses, Manila Southwoods does not cut lakeside vegetation, and the natural growth provides nesting and breeding habitat for amphibians, fish, and birds – more than one hundred species of birds have been counted at the two Manila Southwoods courses. This is double the number of bird species that was found on the site ten years earlier, which is one reason the course has been declared a nature reserve by the town of Carrmona and was chosen as a bird release site by the Department of Environment and Natural Resources.

Cheryll Manzano, who is in charge of pollution control and environment at the club and who co-authored *Guidelines for Maximizing Biodiversity on Golf*, explained that the club has reduced annual water consumption by some 25 percent, and also reduced the amount of chemicals and energy.

So why don't more Asian courses follow Manila Southwoods's example?

Well, a significant minority *are* "eco-responsible." For example, IGOLF-International Golf and Life Foundation, a Swiss-based NGO that promoted environmental and social responsibility in golf, recognized 23 Asian courses as Laureate Courses that adhered to an eight-point charter of environmental and social responsibility.

As for the rest, Micah Woods, a Thailand-based turfgrass expert, thinks the problem is that "there is limited environmental information being presented to people in the golf industry in Asia about the environment." Woods, who advises many of Asia's leading golf courses on how to fix their turfgrass problems, adds that Asian golf courses tend to lag behind European and North American courses in environmental terms because "there are very few regulations here – usually no need to do an environmental impact assessment, little regulation of the chemicals and fertilizers applied, few guidelines for the equipment washing and chemical mixing areas."

What follows is a selection of some other Asian courses that are trying to do the right thing.

## Keppel Club. *Singapore*

Friends had told me to look at Singapore's Keppel Club as a standard-setter for responsible operations.

Located near Singapore's southern tip within sight of Sentosa Island, the club was established in 1904, and is the country's oldest club at the same location (the Singapore Island Country Club is older, but has moved since its establishment in 1891). Keppel Club has some four thousand members playing around more than 5,000 rounds a month.

When he took over as the club's president, Edwin Khew instituted a "Go Green" master plan to make Keppel an "environmental standard bearer" and the "greenest" course in Singapore. Khew, a Nominated Member of Parliament, engineer, and industrialist specializing in transforming waste into renewable energy, explains that the plan includes extensive planting of trees and shrubs that encourage birds, butterflies, and animals to reproduce. It also includes waste management, outreach to the community and to members, and "green operations," particularly to institute energy saving and recycling in "back-of-the-house" activities. Such efforts, he says, can also be good for the bottom line – for instance, recycling organic waste and turning it into bio-compost saves the club several thousand dollars annually.

From the elevated open-air restaurant next to the first

tee, I could see how several of Keppel's holes paralleled Berlayer Creek, the last significant mangrove forest in the southern part of Singapore. Desmond Chua, Keppel's deputy general manager, explains that not only does the club work with Singapore's Public Utility Board to manage the mangrove forest, but Keppel Club has instituted awareness programs with upstream residents, and with local schools, to tell them about the importance of this scarce natural resource that lies on club property.

Admittedly, Keppel Club doesn't have much choice in whether or not to be a good environmental citizen. Like all of Singapore's 32 courses, Keppel must adhere to stringent environmental regulations – in Asia only Japan has similarly tough rules.

Of particular importance in Singapore is the maintenance of an independent water supply. Each of Singapore's courses borders on one of the country's fifteen reservoirs. Tan Nguan Sen, director of the Catchment and Waterways Department of Singapore's Public Utilities Board – the national water agency that manages Singapore's water resources – notes that all golf courses must "comply with our stringent pollution-control requirements and adopt good water-conservation practices." Many countries have similar environmental laws, but Singapore is perhaps unusual in that the laws are enforced.

The importance of Keppel Club's green space for nature conservation has been recognized by the Nature Society (Singapore), which, in a 2008 report noted: "Although it is not itself a wildlife sanctuary, it has over the decades of its existence become increasingly indispensable as a wildlife corridor ... for birdlife." This endorsement is particularly valued by Keppel Club members since it comes from Singapore's anti-golf conservation lobby, which has vocally opposed new golf courses. Alan OwYong, a consultant in the satellite communications industry and a member of Keppel Club, says

"Things are better now, largely because there is more dia-
logue. Courses are listening to the advice given by the con-
servationists."

✧

## Rancamaya Golf & Country Club. *Bogor, Indonesia*

Draw a circle some 50 kilometers (30 miles) around Indonesia's
noisy, congested, polluted, cosmopolitan capital of Jakarta
(population 13 million and counting), and a golfer can find
36 courses, some among the finest in Asia. Rancamaya is not
only one of the most attractive courses in Indonesia, but it
adheres to a strict environmental policy. Ulrich Hahn, Rancamaya's general manager, points out that native trees were
not cut during construction, and the club maintains the wa-
tershed for several rivers that originate in the foothills of the
nearby volcanoes. In addition, the club uses minimal quanti-
ties of chemicals, uses "gray" water for irrigation, and has put
into place sophisticated waste-reduction and recycling programs.

✧

## Song Be Golf Resort. *Ho Chi Minh City, Vietnam*

This complex, made up of three different nine-hole layouts,
regularly receives awards for sustainable development. The
club approaches conservation on several levels, according to
Bobby Chua, the club's director. In addition to the minimal
use of chemicals, a practice common now to many courses,
Song Be has left extensive non-playing areas in a natural state
– as forests and lakes – to provide wildlife habitat, and waste
is treated on-site to reduce the impact on overloaded public
facilities. Visitors to Ho Chi Minh City know that this part
of the city is heavily industrialized, and Song Be serves as a
de facto nature reserve for the area.

✤

## Gassan Khuntan Golf & Resort. *Lampang, Thailand*

Playing the Gassan Khuntan course in northern Thailand can be a daunting experience – narrow fairways, penal rough, and numerous lakes. But the water hazards that gobble errant golf balls are home to some 1,000 rare giant Mekong catfish, introduced by the owners. This fish, which can grow as tall as a man and weight up to 200 kilograms (440 pounds), is considered "critically endangered" by IUCN and is on Appendix I of CITES. Gassan Khuntan has built some twenty lakes and reservoirs, according to Boonsinun Penpanussak, marketing manager of Gassan, which means "the course is self-sufficient in water and we do not need to tap into ground water. We can even provide water to the local communities during the dry season." The original land on which the course was built was parched, almost a wasteland, and the owners have planted more than 30,000 trees, many of which are indigenous species similar to those found in the adjoining Doi Khuntan National Park.

✤

## Banyan Golf Club. *Hua Hin, Thailand*
## Springfield Village Golf and Spa. *Hua Hin, Thailand*

Banyan Golf Club, located in the up-market seaside resort of Hua Hin, was designed by Thai golf architect Pirapon Namatra, whose other courses include the spectacular Santiburi Samui Country Club on Samui island, and Bangsai Country Club near Ayutthaya (itself a good example of a course that is environmentally friendly, partly because of the design, partly due to the philosophy of the owner, and partly because the operators don't spend an awful lot of money to "over-manage" the course). Banyan Golf Club has committed to organizing an annual environmental review to measure reduction in greenhouse gas emissions, air quality protection, energy efficiency, and wastewater management. According to Mark Costello, the club's director of golf operations, Banyan Golf Club is also developing technology to use solar power to run their fleet of electric golf carts.

Also in Hua Hin, Springfield Village uses a closed irrigation system by which water is supplied from on-course lakes, and rainfall and excess irrigation water is recaptured and piped back to those lakes. Noppadon Thampanichawong, Springfield's head of operations, notes that the club uses innovative irrigation techniques to reduce water quantity and frequency of irrigation – achieved by targeted watering, eliminating irrigation on unused portions of the property, and incorporating weather data into daily and long-term irrigation decisions.

According to Springfield's director, Dr. Tasnawat Sombuntham, "We try our best to minimize the use of fertilizers and pesticides," by using environmentally friendly effective microorganisms, also called EM technology. He adds that the club also provides nesting boxes for birds and bats.

**Phokeethra Country Club.** *Siem Reap, Cambodia*

I returned to Siem Reap in 2007 for my first visit since 2000. I was impressed, a bit startled actually, by the number of new hotels that had sprouted to cater to tourists visiting the region's famed Angkor temple ruins. But I was also surprised to find a modern golf course a half-hour's drive from the main temple complex. Cambodian tourist officials hope that the predominantly South Korean and Japanese visitors will take a day off from admiring the region's famous historic sites and include golf in their holiday plans.

But seasonal droughts are a problem in the region, and in designing the new Phokeethra course, Thai architect Major

General Weerayudth Phetbuasak worked with Sofitel, the resort's managing company, to provide adequate water without harming the ecosystem or jeopardizing the water supply of local farmers. He created 19 lakes to collect rainwater for irrigation, and a pumping system to channel the water through all the water hazards on the course. According to Didier Lamoot, general manager of both the golf course and the Sofitel hotel in Siem Reap, this system eliminates the need to drill bore holes (which would diminish the water table and take water away from local users), and might even provide a surplus that could be distributed to local communities.

Lamoot adds, "We are convinced about the importance of maintaining a healthy golf environment." The golf course, like the hotel, plans to generate electricity with solar energy.

Phokeethra Country Club also engaged in some clever public relations. During construction, the builders excavated an 11th-century bridge, dating from the Khmer period. It is government law that all such sites must be protected, so the developers really had no choice about whether or not to look after the structure. But Phokeethra turned this obligation into a positive marketing tool. The Roluh Bridge has now been declared as a UNESCO preservation site. The structure has become the club's logo and led to the course's slogan, "Tee-Off from the 11th century and finish your round in the 21st Century."

**Laguna Phuket Golf Club.** *Phuket, Thailand*

Like most of the golf courses on the holiday island of Phuket, Laguna Phuket Golf Club was built on an abandoned tin mine, an example of "restoration ecology" in which a wasteland is turned into a productive and attractive resource.

Built in 1992, the course includes an "environmental area" that serves as a de facto nature reserve. The Laguna course uses gray water from surrounding hotels, making it self-sufficient in water. Designers have also planted native grasses to reduce the need for fertilizers and chemicals for weed control, according to Tim Haddon, Laguna's director of golf. Haddon feels this is "an effort to rehabilitate and beautify a spoilt, barren piece of land into something useful that both people and fauna can enjoy and benefit from."

Suwalai Pinpradab, director of the Tourism Authority of Thailand Southern Office, interprets this view as a marketing strategy. "With increasing global competition to attract visitors, we feel it is important for Phuket to be seen as a 'green' destination," Pinpradab notes. "But the perception has to reflect the reality, and so we are running workshops for the five golf courses in our region so they can improve their environmental practices."

❖

## New Kuta Golf Club. *Bali, Indonesia*

Sitting on the dramatic limestone cliffs of southern Bali, this 18-hole course opened in November 2008.

Building a course in one of the most arid and unfertile regions in Bali – the area used to be where Balinese prisoners were sent – presented several challenges that reflect the concerns of some environmentalists. Should the region be left alone (good for goats, not much else), or should it be "improved," both environmentally and socially? If the latter, how could changes be achieved most sensitively and effectively?

Because there is little ground water, Made Putrawan, president director of Bali Pecatu Graha Ltd, the owner of the New Kuta Golf Club course, noted that the group built a desalination plant, at a cost of $ 1.7 million, which provides some 3,000 cubic meters (106,000 cubic feet) of water a day. Surplus water is provided free to the local community. Also, some 500 people from the three nearby villages have been employed, accounting for virtually all of the workforce.

"The area is all green now," points out Putrawan, who adds that part of the course will be made into a botanical garden.

The course architect, Ronald Fream, adds that the dry wind-swept site provided several environmental challenges. "We adapted to saline and thin soils. We planted limited golf turf. We protected and preserved the adjacent natural, almost desert-like vegetation. Where possible we planted native trees that are found in this special environment, with a 'semi-Scottish' rough of existing shrubs, long grass, and creepers."

Keeping all those positive indications in mind, I adjust my grip, sight my target, and get ready to hit my tee shot on Manila Southwoods' challenging 17th hole. My drive has to carry a fish-rich pond, fringed with bulrushes. My style may not be perfect, but my eco-karma is fine as I hit a guilt-free drive.

# SUGGESTIONS FOR THE
# UN-WARM, THE UN-FUZZY

## What could golf course owners
## and tax authorities do?

—————◦◦◦◦—————

## BANGKOK, Thailand

F RANKENSTEIN'S MONSTER. VAMPIRE. DARTH VADER. Lord Voldemort. Scrooge.

The world loves a good villain. It's the essence of drama – the badder the villain the gooder the good guy.

And some great villains aren't completely bad; they merely have undeveloped good sides that haven't been exposed to fresh air and the right education.

I suspect that if you did a survey asking whether golf course owners and government tax authorities are good guys or bad guys, the perceptions would be overwhelmingly negative. Neither group is warm and fuzzy.

What might golf course owners and tax authorities do to become eco-golf heroes?

I suggest they acknowledge that a good golf course can be good for nature and take appropriate steps to do the right thing.

But why do so few owners and government officials take a positive view?

The first reason is that in many cases golf course owners

don't *have* to be eco-friendly. There may be no appropriate laws or regulations, and if there *are* laws, the regulations might not be enforced. There is little pressure from the media, from members (who want their fairways as green as Augusta National), from local authorities, from conservation groups. The result: inertia to continue doing the same thing, which is to maximize profits and to hell with "luxuries" like conservation.

Say what you will about over-regulated Singapore, but the country makes sensible environmental laws *and* enforces them. Most of Singapore's golf courses are built adjacent to water catchment areas. Water security is a major security issue in Singapore, which dreads the possibility that neighboring Malaysia, from where approximately forty percent of Singapore's water comes, might turn off the tap. The Singapore Public Utilities Board insists that golf courses protect the water catchment area by maintaining vegetation, by not using many chemicals and providing some public recreational access. The second reason is lack of practical information. Some owners and directors *want* to do better, but don't understand how to reduce pesticides, for example, or how best to plant trees to improve biodiversity.

The third reason is that course directors don't understand the financial incentive they can gain. Grace Fernandez, Manila Southwoods Golf and Country Club's organization development manager, notes that the club has reduced its waste disposal costs by 75 percent during the period 2000–2008 through recycling efforts. And just by "naturalizing" some 48 hectares (118 acres) of the property, the course was able to save $10,000 annually on fuel, labor, pesticides, fertilizers, water, and equipment operating costs.

Fourth, golf course owners and directors aren't very clever at mobilizing public opinion. Conservation groups, community groups, sports associations, and even media can be good allies. Instead, many golf course owners retreat into

a defensive fortress mentality. Instead of positioning themselves as white knights defending the eco-future and taking
pride in being environmental stewards, they allow themselves, by virtue of their silence, to be perceived as the black
demons of destruction.

I find this curious and frustrating, since simply by existing, some golf courses are doing good, particularly in urban
areas. Golf course architect Ronald Fream points out that a
golf course can regenerate a garbage dump site or mining pit,
control erosion, and act as a natural treatment facility for effluent water. Fream, whose design firm GolfPlan – Fream, Dale
& Ramsey has worked in Asia for more than 30 years, even
points out the relevance to climate change, noting that a
"typical" 18-hole golf course turf area generates enough oxy-
gen to support around 8,000 people, and ten trees planted on
a golf course removes the carbon dioxide generated by approximately ten cars. This can result in a substantial carbon
offset, since he adds that "on occasion we plant 2,000 or
3,000 trees around 18 holes."

Finally, there is little incentive from Asian government
tax authorities, which often charge golf courses at the highest tax rate, the same rate for casinos and massage parlors,
because golf is perceived as a (naughty) luxury. Christine
Wiradinata, secretary general of the Indonesia Golf Course
Owners Association, feels that local governments tax golf
courses at the same "luxury" rate as casinos because officials
are not aware of the environmental and social benefits that
golf courses provide to the community.

Curiously, golf courses in America do get tax easements
for environmental stewardship but do not always take advantage of the tax credits available. A 2005 survey found that
only about one in five respondents planned to use conservation easements.

To become eco-golf heroes:

*Golf course owners* should:

- Adhere to the charter of groups that promote and monitor best environmental practices.

- Review all aspects of their operations – energy use, chemicals, water quality, water consumption and supply, biodiversity, and waste management.

- Be imaginative in trying new technologies, like converting agricultural waste into biogas, thereby saving money on waste removal and generating free gas for cooking.

- Seek independent evaluations and take concrete steps to improve weaknesses.

- Use science to fight incorrect perceptions.

- Calculate the monetary value of important, but difficult-to-quantify benefits such as carbon sequestering, providing the community with a de facto nature reserve, air and water filtration, and recreational facilities, then contrast these environmental benefits to the situation that would occur if the land were transformed into, say, a housing estate.

- Respect and enhance cultural and historic sites.

- Treat employees fairly.

- Explain what they're doing and become part of the public debate. Actively seek partnerships with community groups, conservation organizations, sporting authorities, and tourism authorities. Explain the facts. Don't bullshit. Don't hide.

*Government tax authorities* should:

- Adapt a longer-term view of land use and consider the values of good golf courses, particularly when compared to alternative land uses.

- Recognize the difficult-to-calculate values of a golf course, like water retention, carbon sequestering, temperature reduction, or the amount it would cost the government to create a similarly productive nature reserve.

- Offer golf courses that show evidence of environmental responsibility a tax rebate or lower tax rate.

# WHERE HAS YOUR GOLF BALL BEEN?

Taking golf personally.

———◦◦◦———

## DUBLIN, Ireland

**K**ISSING YOUR GOLF BALL CAN BE HAZARDOUS TO your health.

An Irish golfer in the 1990s came down with an unaccountable case of hepatitis. The illness was a mystery to his physician, Dr. Conor Burke, since the patient, a respectable retired engineer, had not been to exotic lands nor partaken of exotic food.

Finally the golfer, a 65-year-old widower who played daily, admitted that he had been licking his ball in order to clean it. Burke surmised that the herbicides and fertilizers used on the greens had infected the unfortunate golfer.

"Some golf course chemicals are cousins of Agent Orange," Burke noted. "Such chemicals are quite toxic to the liver." The physician even invented a new term for the condition: "golf ball liver."

It is one of life's motherly maxims, dating from the early day of childhood: "Don't eat that! It's dirty. You don't know where it's been."

Do you know what kinds of chemicals are used on *your*

golf course? Chemicals don't have to be ingested only through oral contact with an infected ball, of course. The poisons can seep into the water supply as well as into plants.

Whether or not you kiss your golf ball, it makes sense to know the environmental realities of the course you play and help to improve things.

I worked for global nature conservation and health groups for half my life. The reason that environment and health issues are today on the agendas of voters, taxpayers, businesses, and government is because people cared. People said, "We demand a change." In short, people learned about the subject and how it affected them, and then they spoke out.

Sustainable golf is just like politics. Nothing gets changed unless people become educated, raise their voices, and demand change.

Don't leave it to the golf course owners and directors to do the right thing. Some owners and directors are good folks who run sustainable courses. Some are basically good folks who simply haven't thought about it, or don't know how. Some want to do something but are afraid it will cost them money. And then a few golf course owners and directors are greedy, selfish bastards who simply don't care, unless you force them to care. Congratulate and encourage the good guys, scold/teach/blackmail (whatever is your personal style) the bad guys.

And seek eco-golf-karma points, described in the next chapter.

# COLLECTING ECO-GOLF-
# KARMA POINTS

Even though they might be unredeemable,
14 tips to self-serving salvation.

---·———❦❧———·---

## BANGKOK, Thailand

R ELIGIONS PROPOSE A TANTALIZING BARGAIN. "BE-
lieve in our holy teachings, follow our commandments,
and after you die you will be rewarded."

It is this risk-reward that I find so curious, so tempting,
so one-sided.

In golf we face risks with immediate feedback. If I attempt to hit a drive over the lake at an ambitious angle, I will
have immediate feedback – either the ball carries the lake or
it doesn't.

But with religions the reward is not redeemable until I
die. And even then it's not a sure thing. It all comes down to
whether I believe their deal or not. If I am bad in this life will
I go to some form of hell? If I'm good, will I go to some form
of heaven? It's the biggest bet I'll ever make, and I'll never
be able to report back to the still-living whether I won.

So, I believe. Or not.

Most people expend much of their energy accumulating
metaphorical karma points like frequent flyer miles, to build
up their account for an afterlife reward.

On a more mundane level, well-intentioned folks promoting conservation- and health-related issues tell me to change my lifestyle and modify my behavior in order to recoup various rewards.

I've spent much of my professional life working in advertising, and then in senior international positions with the World Wildlife Fund (WWF) and the International Osteoporosis Foundation (IOF). I was a purveyor of the Big Unprovable Promise.

In the advertising agencies at which I worked, I convinced people that this deodorant would make them confident, that this car would make them popular, and that this bank would make them successful. In the mid-1970s, I started to lose interest in advertising. I was working for an ad agency in Jakarta, Indonesia, and during my free time I liked to explore the country. One weekend, a friend and I trekked to a new village created by the government to resettle a group of Baduy. Although they live in *über*-crowded, and increasingly sophisticated Java, the reclusive Baduy have a well-earned reputation for choosing to live far from towns and for rejecting government entreaties to "join the modern world."

At their strictest, the so-called "Inner" (or "White") Baduy have prohibitions against wet rice agriculture, fertilizers, telephones, electricity, traveling in motorized vehicles, raising four-legged animals, using metal farming implements, perfume, hair-cutting, touching money, and wearing anything other than their white homespun clothes. They are masters of magic, and sophisticated Jakartans tell of how former-President Suharto, a staunch believer in mysticism, asked the top Baduy shaman to come to the presidential palace in Jakarta for a consultation. The shaman told the president's intermediary: "If Suharto wants to see me he can come here, in the mountains." And the president, not known for his athleticism or for relishing the outdoor life, made the trek into the steep forested hills southeast of the capital. The "Outer" (or

"Black") Baduy, which includes the few families I visited in the resettlement camp, live a somewhat more relaxed, but still isolated and suspicious life. I'm not quite sure what the government authorities offered these folks, but on the night we stayed at their spacious new bamboo community center in the resettlement village, several dozen Baduy and their two European guests gathered around a communal TV, run by a kerosene-powered generator, to watch Indonesian soap operas. One of my commercials came on screen, selling Trebor sweets, and the group watched with interest. Another of my commercials came on, this time for Pepsodent toothpaste. And a third, for Kraft cheese. Now there is nothing inherently wrong about sweets, toothpaste, or cheese, nor am I against capitalism, but I felt somehow unclean for introducing a commercial "I want it, I need it, and I must have it now" mindset to these simple folks, who were awkwardly trying to decide whether they liked the modern realities of the 20th century.

In conservation our job was two-fold: to get people to change their behavior – use less energy, stop polluting, refuse to buy ivory or wear furs of endangered animals and so on – and also to get the public to believe that "We at WWF are successful, we can do the job for you, so send us money." The payoff was in the far distance – do this for your children so they will have a green world in which to grow up, a world with clean water and pure air and gorillas.

In the health field the message was more directly self-serving. If you don't take care of your body, you will become crippled and incapacitated and become a drooling burden on your family. But the good news is that you can take the tests we offer, and, best news of all, take medication that our big pharmaceutical company sponsors produce, to reduce the threat of brittle bones. This trade-off was sensible and easy for a middle-aged woman to accept because she could see the effects of osteoporosis around her, and she knew that she could do something positive for herself. In any case, who could argue with a lifestyle that encourages someone to see a doctor regularly, exercise, get fresh air, eat leafy greens and not to drink heavily or smoke?

Through it all, our paternal inclination at the advertising agency, or at the non-governmental conservation and health organizations, was to lecture people. "We know best. We're scientists and doctors and we are smarter than you are. Do what we say, for your own good and for the good of the Earth."

But lecturing is bad marketing – it seldom works. Few people enjoy being badgered by a stranger who acts like an overbearing drill sergeant.

We learned that the only way people will act is if they see some sort of reward.

The original version of this chapter listed fourteen things each golfer should do, which could be incorporated into a Charter of Personal Responsibility for golfers.

Doesn't that sound like hard work?

So I've reframed the fourteen suggestions into an opportunity for golfers to earn eco-golf-karma points. I have no idea how the golfer will redeem these points. But I believe that these are things that each golfer can do and might want to do, because they will add to his/her enjoyment of the game while making the Earth a little bit better. There's no guarantee of paradise here, just the opportunity to do a bit of good.

So, with the humble request to consider these suggestions as good/fun/useful/self-serving, here are my Fourteen Tips to Earn Eco-Golf-Karma Points.

1.   EXAMINE your own behavior. Can you reduce the impact of your individual eco-footprint?

2.   ACT on the course. Don't litter. Pick up other people's litter. Don't tolerate eco-abusive behavior in others.

3. WALK. The single most important thing an able-bodied golfer can do. At my home club, Maison Blanche in Echenevex, France (near Geneva, Switzerland), almost all golfers, including most able-bodied males and females over 60, walk. To make their lives a bit easier, many use pull carts with small electric motors. By walking you'll be reducing pollution. But more importantly, walking keeps you fit. Gives you time to plan your next shot. Assists you in seeing the course. Gives you the chance to "investigate" (see below). Helps you enjoy being outside. There's no easy way to say this – golf buggies are for wusses and old guys. (Bonus points: carry your clubs – and you don't need all 14.)

4. INVESTIGATE. Look for areas where grass doesn't have to be cut and where new trees can be planted. Appreciate how abundant biodiversity requires a variety of flora and fauna – those palm trees might look nice but aren't much good for birds and animals. See where riverine vegetation should be left alone and not cut to "look clean." Bird watching can be fun – keep a list. Does the club recycle organic waste, plastic, and glass? Take note of how garbage is disposed of, whether machines leak oil or spout fumes. Talk to the maintenance guys.

5. ASK whether the course has an environmental policy. Read it. Make suggestions to improve it. Insist that the club institute an annual environmental review.

6. TALK. Be proud of your club's environmental credentials. Tell your friends. Tell the media. Encourage the club to include environmental activities when they have tournaments and events. Help design information panels and newsletters

about the wildlife on the course and the club's environmental efforts.

7. ACCEPT that "perfect" golf courses, like the ones you see on TV every weekend, often come at a high environmental price – they might be green because of excessive use of scarce water, or too many chemicals. Sometimes brown is better.

8. POKE around in the back. How does your club manage machinery and agricultural waste? Worker safety? Are chemicals applied in correct dosages and do the groundskeepers wear protective clothing? Has the club instituted new technologies to reduce energy, or biogas systems to convert organic waste into cooking gas?

9. COMMUNITY is important. What's the relationship of the club to the local community in terms of hiring, and social support? Was the land obtained legally and ethically? Does the club support cultural and historic sites? Are there public access footpaths or other recreational opportunities for non-members?

10. JOIN organizations that support nature conservation and golf.

11. LEARN the rules. Learn how to keep score.

12. DON'T BE A JERK. Follow golf etiquette. It's like English grammar – things we already know, like "use active verbs," but that we sometimes forget. Fix your pitch marks. Fix the other guy's pitch marks. Play fast, ready golf. Don't walk on someone's line. Lay the flagstick down gently. (Arnold Palmer's Ten Rules of Golf Etiquette is a great tutorial.) And turn off that damn cell phone (better yet, keep it in the locker).

13. BE HAPPY. Playing golf is much better than not playing golf. Stop whining. Say hello to the gardener. Pick a few (unendangered) flowers for your spouse while in the forest searching for your ball.

14. PLAY FAST, BUT SLOW DOWN and enjoy being in nature, away from the office. Play by the rules. Tell politically incorrect jokes. Bet. Do your best to win. Make every shot count. Breathe.

# WHAT DOES THE
# FUTURE HOLD?

The eco-spiritual golf trend ten years from now.

---

## BANGKOK, Thailand

L IVING IN ASIA FOR MORE THAN HALF MY LIFE HAS
taught me that the only constant is the seesaw juggling
act between tradition, stability, and stasis on the one
hand, and the inevitability of change on the other. This
search for equilibrium forms the basis of Asian life, and the
opposites are everywhere. Indeed, concepts only exist and
take clear form when they are pitted against something they
are not. We define things by what they aren't. Yang is defined by not being yin (although each contains elements of
the other). Male and female. Day and night. Sunny season
and rainy season. Garuda and Naga. Happiness and sadness.
Insight and ignorance. Muhammad Ali and Joe Frazier. New
York Yankees and Boston Red Sox. Heaven and hell. Rich and
poor. Good and evil.

Golf, too, is faced with a battle of contrasts – elitist or
popular, environmentally friendly or environmentally damaging,
relaxing or stressful.

And golfers are also frustratingly schizophrenic. A survey
of 5,000 Canadian golfers indicated that 96 percent enjoyed
seeing and hearing wildlife while playing, and that 90 percent

wanted golf courses to increase naturalized areas for wildlife. Paradoxically, 49 percent of respondents said they still prefer putting areas, tees, and greens to be flawlessly green.

Nevertheless, golf will continue; it is too firmly entrenched, and too many people like it (and too many people make money from it) for the sport to go away.

But change will also come, due to environmental considerations and pressures.

Questions of appropriate land use will continue. A golf course requires some 80 hectares (200 acres) of open space. From an environmental point of view, would this space be better for nature if it were a golf course or if it were turned into an industrial park, a shopping center, or a farm? And since golf courses are built on private land, should there be restrictions on how the terrain is developed?

While predicting is a tricky business, here are some educated guesses about what we might see in the next decade.

## Green Guidelines Will Increase in Importance

Numerous groups involved in golf and nature conservation now promote environmentally sensitive golf course development by providing guidelines and certification programs; these schemes will increase in number and sophistication.

The various professional golf tours will also make adherence to these guidelines a prerequisite for holding a tournament on a particular course, as was the case when European Commission President Jacques Santer endorsed Valderrama, Spain, as the host of the 1997 Ryder Cup because the course is eco-friendly.

And a small, but growing number of golf tourists (notably from northern Europe) will seek courses that offer a wonderful golf experience *and* a commitment to nature.

## Eco-Ratings Will Become Standardized

Just as the handicap system is universal and there is more or less general agreement about the rules of play, we might similarly see a universal eco-grading system.

Courses commonly use the "slope rating" to indicate how hard a course is to play. Although it will be much more difficult to calculate, and likely to be subject to vigorous debate, a parallel rating system could be devised that indicates a course's "green rating."

## Multi-Purpose Golf Courses Will Flourish

While the primary objective of a golf course is to support golf, courses will also recognize that they can meet other needs without sacrificing the quality of play.

Golf courses will become important de facto nature reserves; perhaps even open-air zoos. Most golfers revel in seeing deer wander around the course. Golfers in Florida are used to being told not to go too near the water hazard because of aggressive alligators. Nervous lionesses guarding their cubs sometimes force courses in South Africa to close. The best place for bird watching in Singapore is around the reservoirs that run through the Singapore Island Club's courses. The bottom line is that wildlife likes an eco-friendly course. And golfers like wildlife. (Except for Hawaiian golfer Terry Purpus. His home course on Maui was home to a group of *nene*, the flightless Hawaiian goose. Purpus, 53, became enraged when a *nene* got in his way during a round on Maui, and he whacked the bird with his 7-iron, killing it. According to an Associated Press report, Purpus was fined $4,000 for killing an endangered species and ordered to perform 300 hours of community service.)

✧

Courses will also increasingly provide public access via walking and jogging paths. In some communities, they will be forced to do so by law; in other areas, the courses will open up in search of good community relations.

✧

When cultural and historic sites are on golf courses, as the Moghul tombs on the Delhi Golf Club, the local authorities will recognize that the course can provide professional (and free to the government) stewardship of these national heritage sites.

## More Imaginative Conversion of Wasteland to Golf Courses

As pristine land becomes scarcer, golf course developers will become more imaginative and build courses on wasteland.

✧

The Laguna Phuket Golf Club in Thailand, for example, is built on the site of a former tin mine, while the $20 million Jack Nicklaus-designed Old Works Golf Course in Anaconda, Montana, was built on the grounds of a now-defunct copper smelter that was one of the country's largest and most reviled Superfund sites. "Heck, we've got herons in the water and deer eating the apples," says Derf Soller, superintendent of the Old Works Golf Course. "You didn't see that before. We put up twenty bluebird boxes, and there's a gal who comes out regularly to survey the eggs."

✧

The site of the Widows Walk Golf Course in Scituate, Massachusetts, was an abandoned gravel quarry, just a wildlife-devoid eyesore of dirt-bike trails, illegally dumped tires, and refrigerators. Today it is as biologically diverse as many nature reserves.

## Innovative Habitat Management

Watch for a boom in research on innovative land-use techniques.

In a research project funded in part by the U.S. Golf Association (USGA), James Howard wants to make water hazards friendlier to frogs. Frogs, with their permeable skin and exposure to both water and land, are particularly susceptible to environmental disturbances, according to Howard, a professor at Frostburg State University in Maryland. He is testing alternative designs in Rocky Gap State Park, about 120 miles (190 kilometers) west of Baltimore, near an 18-hole course under construction. The six experimental wetlands in the rough next to the 15th fairway meet federal requirements for replacing wetlands destroyed by the golf course construction. Some of the wetlands are planted with cattails and other aquatic vegetation to provide cover for amphibians and food for their larvae; three of the ponds are designed to dry up in the summer. "Because of their rich vegetation," Howard notes, "they have the ability to detoxify a lot of the fertilizer and pesticides that get introduced through runoff." Are they as good as the original natural wetlands? Or are they perhaps better?

The USGA has invested some $18 million over the last 13 years on research into pesticide and nutrient runoff, breeding more environmentally friendly turfgrass, learning about alternative pest management, and establishing best management practices.

## Water Treatment Techniques

Fresh water, or more precisely the lack of it, will continue to be one of the major environmental issues of the new century, and course operators will welcome innovations in irrigation techniques and improved grass varieties.

Golf architects building courses in arid coastal areas are turning to salt-tolerant turfgrass varieties that use readily available brackish water, leaving intact valuable freshwater supplies.

The Society of Australian Golf Course Architects notes that the use of secondary treated effluent for golf course irrigation has the added advantage of supplying up to 70 percent of the nutrient requirement needed to maintain "quality" turfgrass, thereby lessening the need for chemical support.

# VI

---

# "OUT OF THE POISON IVY?"

Dreaming of truly distant greens

# HOW GOD DOES IT

Unworldly bounces.

— ⋈ —

## COSMIC COUNTRY CLUB, Nirvana

MOSES, JESUS, AND MOHAMMED WERE PLAYING A friendly game of golf for modest stakes — an after-the-game dinner of roast lamb and vintage ambrosia. On the first tee Moses hits a hook into the rough. Mohammed hits it straight, but short. Jesus steps up, adjusts his robes, takes a swipe, and dribbles the ball about as far as the ladies' tee. Moses and Mohammed start to smirk when a gopher emerges from the adjacent forest, runs to the ball, and puts it into its mouth, like a chestnut. As the gopher starts to run back to its shelter, an eagle swoops down, grabs the gopher in its talons, and flies away toward the green. Suddenly the skies darken, and as the eagle is soaring over the green, a bolt of lightning hits the bird, which drops the gopher, which drops the ball. A minor earth tremor then shifts the earth so that the ball starts rolling toward the hole. At the last minute, it looks like the ball will rim out, but a worm pokes its head out of the grass and the ball caroms off the worm, sliding nicely into the middle of the hole.

Mohammed, a gentleman, says, "Jesus, nice shot."

Moses, a realist, says, "Jesus, you wanna play golf or you wanna screw around?"

Golf's a curious sport that sometimes takes unworldly bounces. The ball doesn't move. The target doesn't move. I don't move. I use expensive, finely engineered equipment. It's generally nice weather. The courses are lovely. I usually play with friends. I don't have a huge angry linebacker trying to knock me on my ass.

And it's something I know I can do. All average golfers like me have had their share of birdies, plenty of pars, and countless tap-in bogeys. I know I can do it because I've done it.

But sometimes it seems like misanthropic gods, demi-gods, aliens, the guy behind *Candid Camera*, and cosmic gremlins are all having a good laugh at my golf game. If Zeus were around today, would he play golf? Would he slice? Would he cheat? Did he have a short game? What about Krishna, or Guru Rinpoche, or Huitzilopochtli, or Buddha, or Ahura Mazda, or Viracocha? Would they assume that they deserve a mulligan simply because they are cosmic big shots? Would they tell politically incorrect jokes? Use a lucky coin to mark their balls? Demand to hit first even if they lost the prior hole? Repair their pitch marks?

Which brings me to Ed Fiori. Fiori won four tournaments on the PGA Tour. His last victory, at the 1996 Quad City Classic, denied a young rookie named Tiger Woods his first title. This would be the only time in his career that Woods would fail to win with an outright 54-hole lead until Y.E. Yang outplayed him in the 2009 PGA Championship.

But Fiori's victory over Tiger Woods is a distraction. More important is that I admire, and share Fiori's philosophy and spirit. "I wouldn't care if I got beat by twenty shots," Fiori said. "I'd still like to see how God does it."

We hope you enjoyed *Distant Greens*. You might like Paul's other books, available from Amazon.com and independent bookstores worldwide:

- *Redheads* (A comic eco-thriller set in Borneo)
- *Curious Encounters of the Human Kind* (five-book series of true Asian tales of folly, greed, ambition, and dreams)
- *Share Your Journey: Mastering Personal Writing*
- *An Inordinate Fondness for Beetles: Campfire Conversations with Alfred Russel Wallace*
- *Sultan and the Mermaid Queen*
- *Eco-Bluff Your Way to Greenism* (with Jeff McNeely)
- *Soul of the Tiger: Searching for Nature's Answers in Southeast Asia* (with Jeff McNeely)

# About the Author

Paul in Mongolia on a packed-earth green
with a permanent cement hole.

**Paul Spencer Sochaczewski** has written 12 books and has had some 600 by-lined articles published in major international publications, including *The New York Times, International Herald Tribune, CNN Traveller, Geographical, Reader's Digest,* and *Travel and Leisure.*

Paul has lived and worked in some 80 countries. He served in the United States Peace Corps in Sarawak, Malaysia (on the island of Borneo), and subsequently lived in Singapore, Indonesia, Thailand, and Switzerland. While with WWF – World Wide Fund for Nature International, Paul created international campaigns to protect rainforests, wetlands, plants, and biological diversity.

He walks his hilly home course (Maison Blanche Golf Club, near Geneva, Switzerland) and carries his clubs. He has a lucky Ganesha charm. Several, in fact. Well, actually, a few hundred.

Visit Paul at:
www.sochaczewski.com